JUSTICE FOR OMAR

DETROIT, MICHIGAN

JUSTICE FOR OMAR

A TRUE STORY OF A SISTER'S RESOLVE, A BROTHER'S REDEMPTION

Published by Book Power Publishing, a division of NIYAH.

Special discounts on bulk quantities of Book Power Books are available to corporations, professional associations, non-profit organizations, universities, and others.

Rasheeda may be contacted at: tawfiqspublishing@gmail.com

ISBN: 978-1-945873-17-1 (Paperback)
ISBN: 978-0-9822215-3-2 (Ebook)
ISBN: 978-1-945873-24-9 (Hardcover)

Printed in the United States of America

www.bookpowerpublishing.com

JUSTICE FOR OMAR

A TRUE STORY OF A SISTER'S RESOLVE,
A BROTHER'S REDEMPTION

by

RASHEEDA IMANI JONES AND OMAR JONES

TABLE OF CONTENTS

To our family and comrades.

PUBLISHER'S NOTE

In "Justice For Omar: A Sister's Resolve, A Brother's Redemption," we delve into the intertwined lives of two remarkable individuals—siblings bound not just by blood, but by the stark contrast of freedom and incarceration. Authored by a brother and sister, this poignant narrative offers a rare glimpse into their divergent worlds, their struggles, and their unbreakable bond.

As you journey through these pages, you'll encounter the raw honesty of their experiences. However, a unique aspect of this collaboration is evident: the sister's voice resonates with a depth and expansiveness that mirrors her freedom, while her brother's sections are often marked by brevity, reflecting the constraints of his confinement. His words, though sometimes fewer in number, echo with profound emotion, underscoring the challenges and complexities of life behind bars.

Despite the physical separation imposed by circumstance, their voices converge to tell a story of resilience, hope, and the enduring power of familial love.

"Justice for Omar" is not just a story—it's a testament to the strength of the human spirit, capable of transcending even the most formidable barriers.

We invite you to embark on this extraordinary journey, where every page is a testament to the enduring bond between brother and sister, and a reminder that, even in the darkest of times, echoes of freedom and love and upliftment can still be heard.

-Zarinah El-Amin, Book Power Publishing

HOW THIS BOOK CAME TO BE

They denied his freedom, again. I was sitting in my car when my brother, Omar called from the county jail. He was sad. He was angry.

I heard the desperation in his voice and I didn't know what to do.

A couple of hours prior, our family had been sitting in a courtroom and heard the words that broke our hearts, again. Omar's evidentiary hearing had denied him any hope of coming home. The kicker was this was the same exact courtroom we'd sat in 20 years earlier when Omar was first sentenced to life. The scene was all too familiar.

We relived the trauma of learning that Omar would not be free.

At this point, it had been 20 years of fighting, and we'd truly thought it was going to be different this time. It wasn't.

During our call, Omar was naturally at a low place. I had always been the rock for my family and I knew he needed something to look forward to, something positive. He needed some type of light in this darkness.

I was hesitant at first and thought it was bad timing to suggest this idea but I suddenly blurted out, "We should write a book!"

I'd always dreamed of writing a book and being an author, but this book would be for US. I wanted us to do this thing together. If his body couldn't be free, at least his words and message could go where he couldn't.

His story, his words.
My story, my words.

And so this is how this book came to be. It was a light in the middle of our darkest time. It's been a challenge, and it hasn't been easy revisiting our traumas and our heartbreaks and our pain. But it's been beautiful too. Through the process, Omar and I have grown closer and I've learned a lot about myself as well.

Our hope is that this book gives you a better insight into this world, the nasty world of incarceration and its effects on everyone involved. I wasn't the one behind bars, but I was in a prison just the same.

This is our humble plea for justice.

–Rasheeda

PREFACE

RASHEEDA

"Justice for Omar!" "Justice for Omar!" "Omar Jones not guilty!" were the words we chanted outside of the Los Angeles Superior Courthouse in the year 1997. Yes, at seven years old I walked amongst lawyers, local news crews, neighborhood gangsters, and a host of family and friends in support of my brother's innocence. At seven years old most kids are at school. Privileged kids are lucky – they might be at Disneyland. As for me, I was witnessing and experiencing something that would have an impact on my life forever.

I am from Los Angeles, California – South Central to be exact. You know, Los Angeles, California. Home of the Lakers, Dodgers, the place where we had a celebrity dictating things as a governor before Donald Trump. Los Angeles is the home of the melting pot, where people of all creeds come for opportunity. Los Angeles, where you are a bus ride away from the beautiful beaches and can stand in the middle of your street and see the Hollywood sign. Where dreams of the rich and the famous really do come true. The same Los Angeles where although you see the Hollywood sign, if you live in the inner city the mere thought of walking the streets of Hollywood is not often even attainable.

You know inner city Los Angeles where drugs, prisons, and cemetery trips are far too common. Where our Black and Brown brothers and sisters are murdering each other over rented land, just as often as the Los Angeles Police Department and Sheriffs are quick to pull out their batons, guns, and get acquitted for their charges (rest in peace Ronald Stokes 1962, Ezell Ford 2014, Ryan Twyman 2019, Dayna Mitchell Young aka Malik 2020). Most importantly a place where some of the most beautiful and resilient people reside in The Jungles (Baldwin Hills District), Inglewood, West LA, Carson, Compton, Long Beach, and Watts. Yes, that Los Angeles.

It was in this city that one afternoon a White male judge dropped his gavel and announced with no empathy, sympathy, compassion, or humility, that my brother was found "guilty" of a crime in which he did not commit and sentenced him to "25 years to life with no possibility of parole" in a California State prison.

I remember vividly the screams and cries of my mother's voice. I also remember the somberness in the courtroom as I looked around to observe others' reactions. Everyone appeared shocked as their eyes filled with disappointment, disbelief, and tears.

My eyes wandered back and forth to make sense of what had just happened. My stomach consumed butterflies, my palms sweated profusely, and I felt really fatigued. Literally sick! I strongly believe that kids really do pick up their parents' energy because my mother appeared to experience the same feeling. I was unhappy because my mother was unhappy and there was nothing that anyone could do to comfort her. She lost her entire world with my brother's sentencing – her first-born, her prince, her brave heart, her son.

Due to my mother's emotional outburst when the judge read the words "25 to life" they reprimanded her and demanded that she be removed from the courtroom and never return. Well, that put my brother into a frenzy. I would like to describe it like a scene from a popular Black film. *Dead Presidents* by The Hughes Brothers. At the end of the movie the judge sentenced the character Anthony (played by Larenz Tate), to life in prison. If you have ever watched the film, his reaction was one to remember. Anthony cursed that judge out good as he expressed his sentiments (as the first amendment allows); and if I recall correctly, so did my brother.

Now by no means am I condoning the cursing of a judge in a courtroom, but when you are locked in a cage, subjected to poverty, injustices, inhumane living conditions, in addition to coming from a broken home, then having your life taken away before it even starts – one has the right to express their emotions accordingly. In the film *Dead Presidents*, the character Anthony was guilty of a crime he committed, but not of his lifestyle, and received a life sentence. While my brother was not guilty of his lifestyle, and innocent of the accused crime, he received the same sentence. Every time I see the last scene of that film it takes me back to that day in the courtroom with my brother. Each time that I am taken back I feel the exact feelings as if I were experiencing it all over again – anxiety, grief, anger, confusion, and fear. Yes, each time.

At the time I was far too young, naïve, and ignorant to understand the language of the courtroom and the hurt of my family, or what it meant for our lives moving forward. Here I was witnessing firsthand a biased, flawed, and racist judicial system, a judge who lacked empathy or cultural competency, and jurors of which none were my brother's peers. It was exactly how the judicial system has been depicted since the beginning of time in our good ol' American history.

"Mommy what's life?" I asked with hesitancy and worry in my voice. I believe I was uneasy because I felt that deep down inside my innocent seven-year-old self was not prepared for the answer.

My mom replied in a very disheartened tone of voice, "Baby your brother will be away from us for a while. We will have to pray every day that he comes home soon."

Again, at seven years old I was trying so hard to understand the concept of "life in prison" while barely understanding the concept of what it meant to truly live or what it meant to die. Everyday my mother instructed and guided my twin brother and I to pray for our brother's return home.

"Now I lay me down to sleep,
I pray the Lord my soul to keep,
and if I should die before I wake,
I pray the Lord my soul to take."

In unison we continued, "God bless Mommy, Daddy, Granny, Paw Paw, Grandma, our whole family, etc."

We would list as many people as we could. People who we held close to our heart. We prayed for our family, our neighbors, and those who had transitioned on to heaven. We'd finish our prayers asking, "And God please let Moe and Leon come home soon."

Every day we prayed to God that our brother would come home and everyday was a waiting game for freedom that always seemed so far away.

California Department of Corrections numbers are numbers and letters that identify someone who is incarcerated. The 5 and 99 freeways are routes that are taken to get to the main prisons located up North in California. Between five to seven pictures per envelope is the max that individuals incarcerated can receive, and having the ability to master three-way calls would save the day. These were all things I had to become familiar with as a kid and share with others who were interested in showing my brother love and moral support.

Instead of my mom sitting down with my twin brother and I to read a bedtime story or review my homework (you know like how some of the privileged kids who were probably at Disneyland accustomed to), she would teach us how to address envelopes to California State Penitentiaries. I did not understand the challenges each person in my family had experienced of having a loved one incarcerated as a child, but as a 32-year-old woman I can attest to my own experience.

My mom may read this memoir and ask, "So are you implying that I was a bad mother by exposing you to prison and writing letters?"

My brother will probably say, "That is what Mom was supposed to teach you! Family is supposed to be there for each other and stick together regardless of the situation, "f*ck the bullsh*t."

I would convey to them both and to the readers that I would do the necessary ten times over to ensure that my brother always received love and support while fighting for his freedom.

MOE

Pre-Twins

In my most vivid memories I can still remember being overly spoiled by my mother's affection, protection, and nurturing spirit. She was a young single mother who did her best to raise and provide for her son. I had been the only child, so we were close to the point where I was overprotective of her and loved every moment spent with her. But as the world turns, life changes imminently when growing up in the crevices of South-Central Los Angeles, whether that be good, bad, or ugly.

My mom being young, she'd taken to the streets working at a bookie joint. The bookie joint was a place where folks would come to hangout, drink, and place bets for horses. Instead of people making a drive to Hollywood Park Racetrack to place their bets it was ideal to just place them with her. This lifestyle and environment were fast and had a great cash flow. My mom loved every bit of it, and it allowed her to provide me the best within her reach. I attended private school, stayed with the latest clothes, and drove fly cars.

The downside to this material status was it came with a price. Between the ages eight through thirteen, I endured a steady absence of my mom's presence. Instead of my mother being as present because of her work lifestyle, my grandma and auntie became my surrogate caregivers. The residence of both my aunt and grandmother had been in an area dominated and controlled by a notorious Blood gang. The influence to become a participant of the Bloods was established early. It was normal being that my family not only lived in a neighborhood controlled by Bloods, but my family's home had also been the hangout spot for homies and the gangsters in my family.

Let's fast forward to the day that changed my life. March 27, 1989. I was 13 years old living on 111th and Baring Cross with my aunt and two cousins. My mom was incarcerated and my dad was absent at the time, so I was a kid in the streets adapting to my environment – while at the same time adopting a doctrine. The doctrine would eventually become my survival pack. Late one evening three of my homeboys and I had been chilling in the car smoking and being curious teenagers. As teenage boys we were talking, laughing, and vibing to the latest track at the time. That was, until in a matter of seconds our curiosity led to us tragically being gunned down by two assault rifles.

The assault rifles killed one of my homeboys instantly and landed me in intensive care in critical condition. Due to my critical condition, the correctional facility my mother was housed at allowed her to come nurture her baby boy as I fought for my life. I learned that I had been shot five times and had only one percent chance of living, but God had a different plan for me. Although God had spared my life, I sat in Martin Luther King hospital for three agonizing months.

I had so many thoughts, like "Why God? Why couldn't I just grow up regularly?" I had seen, heard, and experienced too much so young. I had lost one of my best friends the night of the attack and I lost so much after that. I hadn't even reached high school yet and was facing a world bigger than I could've ever imagined.

With all that was transpiring in my life, there was no counselor that awaited me; no program treatment center or anything relevant that could combat the mental, emotional, and physical pain that I'd suffered. Most importantly, the world had made it difficult for my parents, which made it difficult for me.

So I said, "f*ck everything" and turned to the ones who I related to, who cared for me and who I knew had my back. After my physical healing process, I vowed to become one of the most active members in the history of the Bloods. In that moment, my mom knew she'd lost me to that vow.

The Twins "90"

My mother asked me one day, "Moe, how do you feel about having a little brother or sister?"

I replied, "Don't care, I don't want one."

She then replied, "Well get prepared because I am pregnant with twins."

I shot some of my coldest eyes at her, then asked, "By who?"

She says, "Who else, your father?." I couldn't believe it, my mom knew I regarded this man with disdain.

"Mama," I remember shouting, "this n*gga hasn't done sh*t for us why would you do this?" She rebuffed by expressing that she couldn't lose me to an early grave, so she wanted another child; and only by the same man.

It took me some time throughout her pregnancy to finally accept the reality. At 14, I was knee-deep in the streets but I was still a mama's boy. It had always been just my mom and I, but I knew that with my involvement in the streets she desired more children, out of fear that she would lose me.

Because of my love for her and wanting to see her happy, I sucked it up and became my mom's emotional support. I knew the emotional support would be necessary seeing it was only us. And before you know it, I was beyond honored to welcome my siblings into such a cold world, but a warm home that our mama's love brought.

Unfortunately, in our world, our streets, and our game – what goes around comes around; where dues must be paid, karma is real, and nobody is exempt. From the birth of the twins until being incarcerated in 1997, I loved and cared for my brother and sister in the same way I would my own. My mission was to protect them from seeing and hearing the same evils I'd personally experienced.

The years 1996-97 were the beginning to an end for a lot of friends in my neighborhood. Federal agents had eyes on some of them while our rival neighbors had eyes on the others. Reality set in that things would shift for me when I received the phone call that my relative, who I looked to as a big homie and uncle, had been apprehended. I knew in my gut and mind that I was on borrowed time. He had been like a father to me, and it hurt to see him being taken away on a federal indictment because we knew the time that came with it.

He'd taught me a lot, and in my heart, I felt my chances to remain free or alive were slim to none. He had a way of keeping me balanced and grounded. Without his presence, I was bound to act a fool, and one thing about the streets is that they are always taking note.

In our hood we had the LAPD homicide and crash units as our shadows. The Community Resources Against Street Hoodlums (CRASH) was a specialized unit within the Los Angeles Police Department (LAPD) tasked with combating gang-related crimes from 1979 to present day. They were established in the South Central District of Los Angeles.

The Downfall

Being exposed earlier than the average teenager made it appear as though I was living the life. I had the women, nice cars, persona, demeanor, and the look. I was experiencing things that gave individuals the impression I was older than I was. My outgoing personality allowed me to venture into other parts of Los Angeles; primarily areas like the Jungles, Brims, CMG, APB, and 20s. My ventures also gave the police the perfect opportunity to get familiar with my cars, name, and face.

Southwest, 77th, & Southeast Police Departments seem to all have been in collaboration to get me off the streets and imprisoned. I will always believe this to be the case. The cold set up came September 30, 1997, when three CRASH officers arrested me on 9th Ave in the 50s and hauled me off to a homicide substation at the Crenshaw Mall.

Upon my arrival at the police precinct I was escorted to a holding cell, when another detective asked the arresting officer, "whose he?"

"Mad Moe." the arresting officer replied. The detective was an older White male, burly, with a scar protruding across his entire face. I assumed the scar had come from a gunshot wound.

The detective said, "Oh Mad Moe, I was working on a murder case last year involving your Chevrolet Caprice, didn't have enough evidence."

I gave him a cold stare because the fool was mocking my new arrest as if to say, "I didn't get you, but my comrades finally have you."

It's so easy to enter the belly of the beast, but so hard to get out of it.

Bounty Blues

Purple wristband Jones # 5_ _ _ _ _ 187 was my daily reminder of the death penalty I faced for 2 bodies and 1 attempted murder. I can't describe to you how it feels to be accused and reminded of this daily, but I want you to try and imagine.

Usually, the color of the wristband signifies the severity of one's charges. It took me about two months to adjust to my new living conditions and accept the fact that these White folks were serious this time. They wanted me off the streets and it seemed they were willing to do anything to ensure that happened.

Regardless of my innocence and no knowledge of the crimes held against me, the police were adamant about seeking the death penalty or giving me life without the possibility of parole. Again, imagine how that must feel.

I've always counted my blessings, and remain thankful and grateful for having a core of strong individuals who banded around me in dire times. I sat in the county jail for two and a half years fighting for my innocence with a paid lawyer, commissary, supportive family, my girl, and friends – but with a heavy heart.

A different roar echoed through my body, as reality settled in. I unfortunately lost my case in October of 1999.

The Verdict

Anyone who had been familiar with my court proceeding would probably gamble money that my trial was going to end with an acquittal due to the one witness, the lack of evidence, and the sole fact I was innocent of the charges against me. I had a lot of faith in God, my prayers, and myself and I felt God wouldn't punish me like that. My faith was about to be tested.

Before I knew it, the bailiff came to get me from the holding cell but something in my spirit wasn't sitting right. The bailiff's body language sent me into a frenzy of questions.

"What's the deal?" I recall asking.

He retorted quickly, "no idea."

When I made my entrance back into the courtroom, I immediately recognized how the sheriffs formed a line securely alongside the courtroom walls, which to me implied I'd been found guilty. Imagine how that feels.

The sheriff's presence was strong inside the courtroom to maintain order just in case things got out of control. They made the right decision because the courtroom was soon filled with raw emotion coming from those who had believed, fought, and prayed for justice in my name.

After the reading of the verdict, I had to be subdued. Imagine how that feels. I don't remember much of the feeling, but what I will never forget is hearing my mama yell out the most agonizing scream I've ever witnessed. I was her baby and she had been the queen of my throne. The judicial system had just torn at that relationship more than the streets had ever done.

The pain of my mother paired with the guilty verdict had me in shock, but to hear my mama cry like that is what ultimately woke another monster in me. I went back to the holding tank extremely at loss for words. I don't recall the time frame of how long the next court hearing took, but this time the judge criticized my mom for her outburst and denied her access into "his courtroom."

The judge did what they do best. He looked past me as though I did not exist and spoke out to everyone else. He sentenced a 21-year-old Black male youth to life without the possibility of parole, plus 25 years to life to be ran consecutively in California State Prison. I have not even experienced life yet. Imagine how that feels.

CHAPTER 1: SACRAMENTO SANDWICHES

RASHEEDA

When I was growing up, we never knew what was next for us. Some kids were used to structure. Monday-Friday you knew you would be in school from 8:00 AM to 3:00 PM. I imagine that after school you would complete your homework, eat at the dinner table with both parents, and then get sent off to your own room to prepare to do it all over the next day. Here is the best part, I imagined that when the weekends would come, those kids would watch cartoons all day, run in and out the house after playing catch with dad, and then prepare for this big Sunday dinner that mother would prepare. If both mommy and daddy were feeling good then, we would go to Disneyland. I will never be over not being able to frequent Disneyland. Wishful thinking.

Despite this not being my reality as a kid, we looked forward to the road trips to Northern California to visit my big brother Omar. Because of my mother's minor arrest history, she was denied the right to see my brother. There were so many moving parts that went into this adventure that were a battle of their own.

For example, if you ever had a criminal record, it was almost impossible to be granted visitation. My immediate family has a history of offenses which eliminated many of them as options of people who could take us. But I remember it being our grandmother, my older relative, or a lady friend of Omar who would take us. No matter who the driver was during the seasons of our visits, they always made sure we were ok.

At the time I did not understand the sacrifices it took to undergo this journey. I vividly remember these memories as if they occurred yesterday. My twin brother and I would get out our new shoes, our black or gray uniformed outfit, and whatever else was needed that we anticipated taking along our "adventure to the prisons." My mom ensured we had everything we needed. California ID (check), birth certificate (check), notarized letter for minors to visit a loved one in a prison (check), and lastly money (check). My brother and I would get excited when my mom would give us a clear plastic sandwich bag full of quarters and gold dollar coins. "Ha ha Mommy gave me $20," I would tease my twin.

"Shut up, she gave me the same, probably more," he'd say as we continued to prepare for our visit.

I was a young girl unsure what a road trip meant exactly, but nevertheless I was happy. What I was not as enthused about was the 10-hour ride up. It was hot or cold and uncomfortable fitting in the rental car, but we enjoyed ourselves as much as we could. As we would ride the freeway, whether it was my twin and I with my niece or just the two of us, we'd sit in the back seat of the rental car entertaining ourselves as kids naturally would. I laugh thinking back how we'd play 'punch bug' as we observed all the different cars, giving one another a playful punch once we noticed the old school Volkswagen Beetle. We thought of ways to entertain one another and ourselves during our long rides to the prison.

I remember one time we used our imagination and storytelling talents when passing up a sign that said, "The Texas Chain Saw Massacre." We were scared but it didn't stop us from trying to scare each other with the possibility of the chainsaw man being real and somehow getting to us on the highway. Not only did we use our imaginations for stories, but we used our physical strength when we played one of the popular kid games, BB Bridges. My twin always took BB Bridges too far. We would use our memory I recall, reciting word for word from the movie *Friday* by Ice Cube, and our rapping car cyphers thinking we all were inspiring rappers. We really were just trying to make the best out of every situation.

I think one of the fondest memories of our experience was the satisfaction of preparing our 'Sacramento Sandwiches' for the road trip. Let me give you a quick fill in. A 'Sacramento Sandwich' is a piece of bread with melted meat and cheese. We called it a 'Sacramento Sandwich' because the night before we would prepare them for our ride up north to Sacramento. It was so simple but with a bag of Dorito chips, it was gourmet.

"Aye, let me get another Sacramento Sandwich" one of us would yell from the backseat. There was always one ready to be eaten.

Most of the road trips included my niece, Omar's daughter. My niece, Omar's daughter, is only three years younger than my twin brother and me. Although we did not grow up in the same home, we all grew up close enough to where we treated each other like siblings. These rides to visit our big brother, her father, allowed us to bond as kids. For her, she thought her daddy was on "vacation" so when she was with us, we were on our way to see "daddy on vacation."

Sitting in the backseat of the car, gaze fixated on everything passing in the freeways, we headed to my brother's place for "vacationing." We'd listen to some of our favorite jams on the way. We jammed listening to Mary J. Blige "Share My World", singing aloud with my niece was always a special moment. We sang as if this classic song belonged to the two of us. I can't forget about Ludacris' *Word of Mouf* album that got us through some rides. Man, despite the circumstances those were some memorable times as kids.

I made the best of the situation I could make sense of, although I wasn't fully aware of the many obstacles my family faced. But I still recall some of the hurdles clearly as ever. I remember after many car drives, the visiting officers would give us the blues, a run for our money, a hard time for no reason. I knew nothing about much, yet one guard said that me wearing my red Rocawear outfit was prohibited. These were CDCR rules. Then another officer requested that I change only for another officer to approve it, because although I was developed for my age, I was still a minor.

"Too tight," "wrong color," it seemed like they nit-picked at everything. It almost took away the joy we experienced on our car ride when met with these foolish rules. From securing finances and mobility, then requesting time away from work just to make these visits possible, the system still made the incarcerated individuals' families endure challenges.

"All clear. They can go in now."

As soon as we got past the bob wire and metal detectors, our anticipated moment awaited us. We were able to see Omar. For the most part we made good use of our $20 that mommy had sent us with. Hot Cheetos, Fruitopias, Starburst, burritos, and hot wings. Uno cards, checkers, and dominoes were amongst some of the games on the table that were there in case we needed to pass time. We all sat around Omar, each time quiet, sometimes shy or not even knowing what to say.

This had been our brother who was now in a place that he temporarily called home. It was an adjustment not to hear him come home late at night with Rally's burgers, or have him ask my twin brother and I for favors. Those days were now only memories. Our reality was us sitting in the visiting room monitored by unfamiliar people in an unfamiliar territory, learning about each other and adjusting to our new lives.

What brought me the most joy, despite the unfortunate circumstance, were those dusty visiting rooms that brought smiles. We would laugh and joke, catching up was always fun. Sometimes, I would drift in my thoughts when I saw my niece joyfully sitting on her daddy's lap. It would make me sad that they could only experience those moments with time constraints and stupid rules. Oftentimes, during the visits it was also a reminder that I never got to experience seeing my daddy on "vacation" or sitting on his lap. I have never talked about how that affected me.

- -

Friday, April 13, 01

Dearest Rasheeda —

Hello my dear loving daughter! :) How are you and the family? I pray that all is well with you. I really miss you and your brother. Waking up at my house and going to school every morning & then coming home again. I had fun with you there with me. I will be home shortly, and we'll be together again. How is school?? You should be ready to graduate pretty soon. I hope you are still into the books - - - you are too young for boys, so remember your dad is watching you!!! :) I'm sorry I'm missing your birthday again, but I can make it up to you in June. ok? Miss Sheeda? Give my love to your bro, mother and Grandma. I will write to you again as soon as I move to another prison and give you my new address. I love you dear!

Happy Birthday on May 1.

Love, Your Father

- -

Friday - April 13, '01

Dearest Rasheeda —

Hello my dear loving daughter! :) How are you and the Family? I pray that all is well with you. I really miss you and your brother; waking up at my house and going to school every morning & then coming home again. I had fun with you there with me. I will be home shortly and we'll be together again. How is school?? You should be ready to graduate pretty soon. I hope you are still into the books --- you are too young for boys, so remember, your Dad is watching you!! :). I'm sorry I'm missing your birthday again, but I can make it up to you in June. O.K? Miss 'Sheeda?? Give my love to your Bro', Mother Cheryle, and Grandma.

I will write you again as soon as I move to another prison and give you my new address. I love you Dear!! Happy Birthday on May 1.

Love. Your father

Most times, those visits were a reminder that my mom cried many nights praying for my brother's return, or to simply have him in her arms again. It was a constant reminder and uncertainty that we experienced what our lives would be like as we grew older.

"Times up. Hug your visitors. Visiting hours are now over."

It was never easy to depart. If I could speak for all of us, it was always awkward and uncomfortable and not a good feeling. We had to leave someone we loved behind in a place that was not designed for people. I'll repeat that; even at my young age I knew that jail, prison, and cells were not designed for people.

We'd drive 20 hours in total, for a loving and needed 2 to 4-hour visit (depending on the number of families who showed up). 10-hour rides there and 10-hour rides back. Our drives home were never as lively as our drives up were. Most times on the way home, we would sleep like we'd just worked a whole shift on our feet. The visits were mentally, physically, and emotionally exhausting, even with smiles.

When we arrived back home in Los Angeles, we unpacked the car, gave each other hugs, and life continued for us. We didn't know what life was like for Omar because we were still young. We couldn't fathom at the time what he experienced when visits were over, but with time, we would all soon find out. We all went our separate ways.

Letters, phone calls, and pictures were our way to stay connected until our next scheduled visit, which would occur when circumstances and time permitted. It's crazy that whenever my niece, brother, and I would meet again, we didn't discuss the thoughts or feelings that we experienced throughout the year; during birthdays and holidays when Omar was not there. We would just reminisce, laugh, and talk about those good ol 'Sacramento Sandwiches.'

MOE

New Folsom was a Level IV maximum security prison located in Represa, CA. New Folsom was close to Sacramento. This was the first prison I landed in, and my first time in the penitentiary. 23-years-old with a life sentence. Usually 'new fish' and first timers are nervous or fearful. The unknown of what awaits you in such a hostile place can either make or break you mentally, which then will determine your physical status and destiny. I'd been doing time since I was fourteen if you consider fire camp and minor run-ins with the law; so mentally and physically, I had conditioned my mind to ward off such odds, fears, and adversity.

I hit the general population comfortably and confidently. I knew a lot of homies who were there and those that didn't know me would soon respect me, because most honorable members respected honorable members. I entered this encampment with a respected name, due to the vow I'd made on the streets. Upon arriving in new territory I immediately let the elders know I was down for the cause. I was willing to show and prove myself however it meant.

Lashing out in anger and hurt came easy, being that I had so much built-up mixed emotions and hatred having experienced the false conviction. Here I was, an innocent young man being stripped of his freedom, and on what truth or facts? This was indeed a hard pill to swallow and accept. While my days turned into weeks, and my weeks into months, I began settling in and getting my priorities together.

A 13-inch television, radio/CD player, clothes, CDs, books, literally anything I thought was worth attaining I purchased. This had been the millennium year of 2000. My old neighborhood was still up and running despite some of the losses in it, and I still managed to receive love and support. Honestly, it was overwhelming to know that I was still remembered and respected. I didn't want or need anything as far as materials were concerned. My mail was pouring in, and phone time wasn't an issue. However, it was time to see who really cared about me to make that drive up north for visits.

I remember I had spoken to my girl at the time. Since being found guilty and leaving the county jail our communication wasn't up to par. Location played a role in our losing connection and we barely had much contact due to limited phone usage. I had gone from being on the phone at my leisure, to not being afforded phone calls as much due to being housed in a reception center.

Once arriving at reception, you'd more than likely spend most of your time in a cell, remaining housed in a reception center until you meet with the counselors, then awaiting departure to a prison where your time would start. When I did get a chance to call her, she seemed different. I can't pinpoint what it had been, but my gut instinct told me something was wrong because our conversation was awkward.

One day I got some news that one of my best friends was killed which left me sick. Days later one of the homeboy's girl exposed the truth that made my instincts prove to be right. She said she saw my girl at my best friend's funeral and asked how many months pregnant was she? If only y'all could have seen my face; sick and mad is an understatement. I told the homie's girl that the police were tripping but I was lying. I needed an excuse to get off the phone so that I could get to the bottom of this. I couldn't wait to get off the phone and call her ass.

When I got ahold of her, she couldn't say anything that would ease the pain, clear my negative thoughts, or give me any reason to forgive her. In my young mind and narrow thinking all I knew was, the girl who had my heart had gone against the grain, which was treason in my beliefs. But for some odd reason I needed her to come visit me so we could see if we were savable because the love was real. So, we scheduled a visit that following weekend. She would accompany my maternal grandmother who we call 'grams'.

The weekend came when I would get to see them both. It had been a while since I'd had any physical touch from those I loved, so I really looked forward to it despite how I felt about her actions. Since my cellmate had been up to date about my relationship antics, when they called me over the loudspeaker for my visit he looked at me and said "go get her champ", meaning clown her ass!

As I entered the visiting room my eyes scanned the entire room searching for my family, thinking to myself "it's crunch time." My heart started beating irregularly as I continued to locate them amongst the other families. I was looking forward to hugging grams but honestly every fiber in me was fixated on mentally abusing this girl. I finally saw grams; she waved me over to the vending machine smiling. I coolly walked up and kissed her.

I immediately asked her, "where is my girl, in the restroom?"

Grams replied, "No, she didn't come. She said something about how she missed her hair appointment." Grams rolled her eyes and said *"Tuh."*

My attitude used to be bad back then, so I immediately start tripping saying, "F*ck her! Go get my car, jewelry, and clothes from her possession."

Grams humbly said, "Boy sit down, calm down, and enjoy the rest of this visit." As she began to dig into the hot wings, she had the audacity to say, "I like her. She gets me good outfits at the mall and therefore I'm out of you guy's business."

I never got to talk about how her not showing up impacted me and I probably never will, but it did. This was just another experience and hurt feelings that I had to charge to the game, especially in this environment. All I could do was suck it up and enjoy the wings with grams.

One thing's for sure that one monkey won't stop the show, the show must go on. My visitor's list was growing but only a few would show face. This was the moment my baby girls started coming to visit me, both my younger sister and daughter. I was thankful for the women who did make sacrifices to ensure I kept a relationship with them through visits.

This girl I had met on the street I lived on, was enrolled in Crenshaw High School. She'd been five or six years younger than me, but she was solid. She started to bring my princesses to come visit me. My girl and I had split and could not reconcile our relationship and honestly it had left me bitter. In this mist of that, I did appreciate the friendships I developed along the way. I'd be lying if I said the bitterness was not from the loss of love, but subconsciously the mishap had disturbed my program in jail. I started looking for trouble, often getting into frivolous sh*t. I didn't care, it literally felt like I had no purpose to do good.

I was at a low point and didn't realize my visitors would wash the sin off my hands with hugs, take the stress away with youthful smiles, and ignite the purpose in me that I needed to live. My family, women friends, and relatives brought light to a dark visiting room. These people were prominent in my emotional and mental state of being, when they could afford the time to see me. The early stages of a life sentence are crucial to the direction of how you do your time; you can do the time or let the time do you. At this point my support system was high but my morale was at a low, with this attitude 'the holes' (As Seg/SHU) became my constant resting place.

- -

Ded: BACK DOWN MEMORY LANE
Minnie Rippleton

Oct 5, 2005-

Lil sis, what it do? ALL AS WELL I HOPE & PRAY. I just received your Kite and flicks today so I'm At CHA LIKE CLOCK WORK. I see you're engaged in a puppy love thang. It's common at your age. I noticed you're emotionally attached somewhat already to this young fellow. That is what I don't like or want because if oh boy your feelings "it don't even have to be purposely" but you're too young to be all upset over a boy. You must stay focused Sheeda. If oh boy treat you cool "respect you" and willing to wait for you sexually, I'm not tripping. Long as you keep your mind on career goals, education, family, and carry yourself like the young queen you are and never settle for less in life especially pertaining to males. You deserve the best so if a young male can't make you laugh, smile and be happy and like you unconditionally (HE'S IN THE WAY).

Yeah fasho I'm gonna have to sidebar with this young character and see where his mind is at, see if he's worthy of having my sista as his female. It's only so much I can say and my actions are limited due to these 4 walls I'm surrounded by. ████████ . I go to committee next week so <u>I should</u> be going back to the mainline. Yes, I'm still in the hole. I finally received my XXL MAG. Yes sis, I am alright just knocking down days, months, and years and educating my mind & discipling the body. Staying busta free always. Tell my boy Rasheed I Said West↑ and keep his head to the sky.

How is mom? Kiss her for me. I send you all my love. I'm truly missing eveyone. A visit sounds good to the ears. I have so much to ask, say, express and so on. I'll call as soon as I get to a phone. Sheeda who is this boy you like folks? Do he have family from the hood? What street does he stay on? How old is he? Are you kissing yet? All that you getting into drama with other girls over blood "No good." You be the bigger person and don't be crying over no nigga . . .I don't like that ------

Tell Curt, Leebee 1 & 2 I said wes and I send them my love! Girl, ya flicks is cool. You're cute. Stop stressing yourself over small shit :) This was a brief kite because I got your mail at night and I am trying to get it back to you A.S.A.P. Be expecting my call sometime this month. Until then b safe, take care, and don't love so easy!

- loving you hard —
yours 4 ever
your brother M-Moe1

- -

ed Φ! BACK down MEMORY LANE — oct 5, 2005 —
minnie Appleton

LL SIS, WHAT it do? ALL AS WELL I HOPE & PRAY. I just received your kite & flicks today so im at cha like clock work. I see your engaged in the puppy love thang it's common at your age. I notice your emotionally attached somewhat already to this young fellow. That's what I dont like or want because if oh boy hurt your feelings "it dont even have to be purposely" but your too young to be all upset over a boy you must stay focused. Sheeda if oh boy treat you cool "respect you" and willing to wait for you sexually I'm not tripping. Long as you keep your mind on career goals, education, family, and carry yourself like the young queen you are and never settle for less in life especially pertaining to males. you deserve the best so if a young male can't make you laugh, smile & be happy and like you unconditional (he's in the way).

Yeah fa sho I'm gonna have to side bar this young caracter and see where his mind at, see if he's worthy of having my sista as his female. It's only so much I can say and my actions are limited due to these 4 walls im surrounded by. ██████████ I go to committee next week so I should be going back to the mainline yes im still in the hole, I finally received my XXL mag yes sis im alright just maintaining knocking down days, months & years and educating my mind & discipling the body, staying busta free always. Tell my boy Rasheed I said west ↑ and keep his head 2 the sky.

Hows mom? Kiss her for me and I send you all my love and im truely missing everyone. A visit sounds good to the ears. I have so much to ask, say, express and so on. I'll call also soon as I get to a phone. Sheeda who is this boy you like folks? do he have family from the hood? what street does he stay on? how old is he? are you kissing yet? All that you getting into drama with other girls over blood "no good" you be the bigga figga and dont be crying over no nigga I dont like that —

Tell curt lewee & I said wes as well and I send them my love! Girl yar flicks is cool you're cute stop stressing yourself over small shit ☺. This was a brief kite because I got your mail at night and im trying to get it back to you a-s-a-p be expecting my call sometime this month until then B safe, take care, and dont love so easy!

██████████

Loving you hard —
yours 4 ever
your brother M-Moe-1

CHAPTER 2:
DEAR DIARY

RASHEEDA

A lot of my time was spent home in the presence of my twin. My mom was at work and my daddy was where daddy was. So it was always just him and I, until he started to become a victim of the "lifestyle." I longed for conversation, discussions with my mom, or anybody who was willing to listen and ask how my day was at school, or what was wrong; but the opportunity for that came far and in between. As you can imagine as an individual that lacked the opportunity to verbally express myself, I developed a comfort in writing letters in my diary.

My diary became my imaginary best friend. I would write about my dislike for World History, my aspirations for what I wanted to be when I grew up, and who my crush was for the week. That was the highlight of my diary. Who was Rasheeda crushing on? So much so that whenever my little cousins would come over to spend time with me, they gathered on my bed requesting to read my diary like it was Word Up Magazine.

My diary was really that good! It was an escape from my everyday reality. I got to be whoever I wanted to be and say whatever I wanted to say freely. I was able to communicate my wants and needs even if it prompted me to shed tears, which I did on many occasions. My dairy was my safe space, and it was what kept me sane.

My diary kept me sane on days when I thought the world was over. Writing was therapy and this small tangible object kept all my secrets in good company. I didn't have a lock; I didn't need a lock. I felt whoever got a hold of it would run into a pot of gold. My diary was full of imagination and dreams, but also truth, vulnerability, and pain. Whoever had a chance to touch it would know this young girl was struggling to balance school, learning what it meant to be a young woman, and battling what love was and was not.

Looking back, as many fairytale moments I had in my life around that time, those moments were no fairytale. They were attachment moments. Moments that I would have never known if my family had been more present. They were moments that I had created in my head as a perfect love story, but it was really what we would call today "toxic."

I was in a relationship with a guy for at least three of my teenage years before I was officially considered a legal age of 18. In those three years you couldn't tell me that my love with him would not last an eternity. You couldn't tell me anything about this love. Not my mom, my dad, or any friend of mine. Surely not any friend of mine. What would they know? What did anyone know? To me this was the most beautiful love story that I was a part of.

I thought it was normal for a hood story to begin and end with jail, drama, amongst other things – like they publicized in the movies. I started the relationship with my love being incarcerated at a camp facility. I can't recall why he was there, but I subconsciously had my mind programmed to write letters, be of support, and be emotionally and physically available to someone who was in jail.

I started writing this love, sending pictures to this love, and planning my life with this love. I smile as I reflect. I had it packed. Five pictures per envelope, a splash of Bath and Body Works, and a sealed kiss with lip gloss to enclose the most heartfelt 3–5 page letters I could send. I anticipated my love and his return from camp so I could be right there with him.

LRG jeans, Air Force Ones sneakers, and a bag of colorful Pro Club T-Shirts with my hard earned $100 that I'd saved from my lunch money was the perfect welcome home gift. I sat in the car with my love's dad, his best friend, and some of his loved ones and we were off to get him. I was elated, excited, and full of bliss to be on the road to go get my love. I had years of experience and years of anticipation awaiting the days and marking the calendar for someone I loved to come home, and I was finally able to see, feel, and taste first-hand what freedom was like. He was free!

I wish I could tell you that my love story ended with a beautiful child, marriage, and me off to college with him on the way at Morehouse (you know like Tray and Brandy in the classic film

Boyz N the Hood). My story is my story and it panned out a little differently. I was a young girl with no experience about anything. I didn't know a drug from a drug. Sex from sex. I didn't really know much. Very naïve and ignorant to a lot of things considering I was right in the midst of it. My family at some point was very familiar with the ropes, and so was my love.

Out of respect, I'll only speak about my experience with him. Most days were heaven, some days were hell, and there were a handful of days where I had an outer body experience. The drama of other girls and other girlfriends became a constant issue. Partying, friends, and insecurities within the relationship started to become the norm. If you listen to the music, watch the television, and look at what I have observed all around me, this was normal and something I could get through. I was my love's "ride or die."

One thing about being a "ride or die" is that you will be tested. The tests are reckless, unrealistic, and unhealthy as hell if you ask me now. You mean I have to watch you lie? Cheat? And receive broken promises just to show him I loved him? What part of any healthy relationship is that? At 17 years old, what did I know? Here I was still just riding, until one day the lines and boundaries were crossed, and my diary became a thing of the past.

I was taking a shower and while I was showering my love grabbed ahold of my diary. If I ever said I didn't need a lock on my diary, Lord knows I wish I had a lock. I left my shower in a great space. I was energized and ready for our daily adventures only to enter a room with my diary, something so sacred and safe, ripped into a million pieces.

My stories! My dreams! My pain! My purpose! My tears! Years of vulnerability and growth ripped into a million pieces.

At that moment no part of me had the energy to put it together. I just stared in a state of shock as the tears rolled down my cheek. I looked up to see a hole in the wall and the resentment in my love's face. He looked pissed! He looked hurt! My notable crushes. It was my mention of my crushes or probably the desire to want more from the relationship, or maybe my ongoing mention of significant male friendships that I'd acquired.

Nonetheless, that was the start of our unhealthy relationship. Where trust, his perspective, and our love were tainted. Once it's tainted, it's tainted. I would like to say we tried. I don't think it was ever the same. The cheating, the lies, deceit, and everything else happened on both ends but somehow the "love" and attachment remained.

I often ask myself why I stayed. The only thing I came up with is a genuine love for him. The love remained but the toxic energy only became worse. This time I had no one to turn to. I couldn't inform my friends; they would judge me. I couldn't tell my mommy because our relationship wasn't as present due to her being at work; plus, she would hate him. I couldn't write it in my diary because well, I never returned to writing or had the heart to write again. Something about that experience traumatized me. I was good. I couldn't turn to my brothers or my dad because they were unreachable. They were all incarcerated.

Essentially, I had no one and my love knew it. He knew that I depended on all of him and a part of me started to despise it. The bond was strong, and I couldn't seem to shake it. As much as I knew I needed to shake it, I couldn't seem to let that stronghold go. For a short-lived time, the dynamic in the relationship became something I always said it would never become. This emotional and mental connection and attachment became a physical catastrophe.

Arguments would almost always become physical, and we would go blow for blow. Punches became slaps and then that became an all-out fight. I could never sit around and just take him hitting on me, which is what it was at first. I felt helpless more times than not. Then, I mustered up some courage. I like to think every wrestling match with my twin brother when I was younger helped prepare me for those moments. I would always imitate The Rock or Stone-Cold Steve Austin, and a part of that practice made me fearless when it came to any physical altercation.

Not to make light of anything related to domestic violence ever. There's just something about experiencing a level of pain that you sometimes become numb to it. I had experienced so much emotional and physical pain during my life that during those encounters the psychological pain afterwards is what hurt most. I had witnessed domestic abuse all around me. I thought it was a way to show my love and deal with it. If we overcame it, it was worth something. I didn't have fear, regardless of how it was going to end. I was prepared, even if it was my impulse or irritability that threw the first hit. Life is about accountability.

Holding myself accountable now is taking ownership for leaving when I left. After several hospital visits, bruises, and lies

I had run out of excuses of what to tell others about my awkward appearance and random bruises. I had to check myself. I had to really look in the mirror to evaluate my self-worth.

"Dear Diary,

Rasheeda you are in school, on your way to college, and homecoming queen. You have a lot of people around you willing to love you, if you let them. You are such a beautiful girl. Why are you allowing yourself to endure this? Don't you feel you deserve more?"

I instantly ripped the diary entry up. As pretty as people told me I was, as much as I attended church, sang in the choir, had so many opportunities at my feet – there was an attention, a love, that I was missing. My daddy, my brothers, my cousins – resentment (cries to self). You guys were supposed to be here.

The Final Straw

The random fights continued. I remember we wore our Sunday best for church. The plan was to go to church and have lunch after. I had on a pretty black lace dress that I had saved up my money for from Forever 21. I had fresh pin curls and my new Baker heels. It was our pastor and his wife's anniversary, and the choir was singing some of our favorite gospel selections for morning and afternoon services.

My love sat in the audience with me after my role in the morning service was fulfilled. I am not sure what triggered him but by the end of the service he was ready to go and all our plans for the day were no more. I reasoned with and begged for him to communicate to me what had happened, but all that did was turn into a huge argument that turned physical while we drove down a busy street. As much as I was upset at God that day, it was only His grace that spared our lives.

The fight was ugly, bad, and sad. I vividly remember crying for help, and no one came. No one ever came. It was like an unspoken rule or something, but people always only watched. I know there is a "no snitch code" and I would never hold that expectation for anyone. I just needed to be saved. That's all I ever wanted, was for someone to see me. To hug me. To tell me and remind me that I deserved more. To ask me where the f*ck were my parents and family, or people who loved me. Yea, no one ever saved me.

The fight lasted until we got to his house which was at least 15–20 minutes from the church. By the time we made it to his house my new laced black dress was ripped up exposing my goods, my hair was sweated out, and I had a knot on the side of my face. My eyes looked like I had a mild allergic reaction from how puffy they were from me crying.

My love's family helped put me back together. Yes, Black women put me back together. Someone sewed the buttons on my dress while another person helped me cover my face and laid my edges back down. I tried so hard to stop crying internally. I was embarrassed, ashamed, and hurt. I needed a hug. I wanted my mommy. God, I just wanted and needed something that I did not have at that moment – love that was present. At that moment, the most important thing was me getting back to church for our 3 PM service.

When I got back to church, I just knew that my life was going to be exposed and I would somehow be looked at as a victim of domestic violence. The energy was off, at least it was to me. How could anyone not pick up on my energy? My niece knew something was wrong. We were connected like that. She didn't utter a word. She just pulled my hair back behind my ears and I knew that was her way of letting me know she knew what had happened. Other than that exchange, no one else said anything or asked anything. They never did.

I washed my face one last time. I took a deep breath, "Rasheeda, don't you cry. You got this!"

I hopped in the choir stand and hopped right in sync.

"How great is our God. Sing with me.
How great is our God, and all will see.
How great, how great is our God."

There was no more my love. Several incidents after I finally let go. I had to. At some point I had to want more for myself. I had to live the life that I'd been preaching. A healthy life. A life that displayed that I loved myself. I became a mentor at random events for youth who come from similar inner city backgrounds. My relationship didn't align with my future and what I knew that God wanted for me. So, I put away the relationship, the diary, and started to lean on a support that was far, but could be near if I wanted.

My brother became my personal diary. Every time I would get into a disagreement of some sort, men's favorite line to shut me up was "go get your brother." I am unsure if it was a slap in the face or to be funny because getting either of my brothers wasn't an option, but I used every opportunity to really lean on my older brother and lean on him fast.

I started to use my time and energy to develop a relationship. I remember writing letters talking about my new love interest, asking for permission to date, and vaguely talking about my desires for the future. My brother had to receive almost 3-4 page letters from me telling him about the three different guys in my life and how much they meant to me. We laugh hysterically when we talk about it now. I gave the run down on their names, demographics, geographic affiliations, and why they were significant in my life. I needed him to know these weren't some fly-by-night guys; these were people at the time that I trusted with my life, and I needed him to be fully aware.

- -

Dedikation: Position of Power by 50 Cent
I ain't gone cry no more by Shareefa

Nov 7, 2006

Supreme love & respect to my lil sis, Sheeda on some real talk, real feelings, can you forgive me for not getting the opportunity to walk & talk "our time." Sis on Lanes I felt way guilty when I went back to my cell due to whatever you had on your mind was just as important & worth than what I had discussed with my daughter and her mom ████████. Sis I love you equally no more, no less than I do Grams, Moms and my daughter ████_I swear yall my everythang. Sis I know your of age where you can take care of yourself but it's a brother instinct to be concerned about you? That is why I asked you who house you were going to after the visit. I'm going to stay in your business as long as I am breathing so get use to it ☺

Sis I am proud to see you keeping yourself together physically. Mentally you're still grinding which I respect to the fullest because studying is straight discipline. The payoff gone be worth it------

Sis I heard oh boy you like is about to come home and I am sure you're under pressure to make a decision (sexually).

I can't call that due to it's on you being on you to decide whose worth receiving something so sacred & precious. I know one thing once you give it up do you think yall be closer? Will he treat you right or you better? Will you be happier? Take all those questions into consideration before reacting.

████████████████████████████ ██████████████ Sheeda I'm a bit more harder on boys yall mess with. I know how YGs think_██████████ ████_So I'm going to always analyze things in depth. Sis you're looking cuter as you age so then men will flock but as long as you stay ahead of the

game people in this wicked world you'll be alright.

Sis don't be so quick to involve your emotions into relationships. If they don't work out it won't be a loss on your end. If you keep it with no strings attached then your expectations won't be that high "You feel me." What I look like letting my lil sis become a victim of the hands of any nigga ███ ███████████████. *It is my duty to lace your boots on all walks of life even though I can't hold your hand through the journey.*

Rasheeda, you have been slacking as well as getting on me about whatever. It's been hard for me to assist you when there is little I'm left with to go on.

Sis, watch over moms, grams, aunty, and of course the young Tropikals ███████.

I love you and miss you already. God's my witness I feel like I'm being cheated not being able to be in yall company. I pray in due time God will free me and throw his son back into yall presence. Until then stay focused sis.

- -

DEDIKATION ₱ POSITION OF POWER .. SOCENT

I AIN'T GONE CRY NO MORE .. SHAREEFA

NOV 7, 2006 ═

SUPREME LOVE & RESPECT TO MY lil SIS, SHEEDA ON SOME REAL TALK, REAL FEELINGS, CAN YOU FORGIVE ME FOR NOT GETTING THE OPPORTUNIT TO WALK & TALK TO YOU "OUR TIME"? SIS ON LANES I FELT WAY GUILTY WHEN I WENT BACK TO MY CELL DUE TO WHATEVER YOU HAD ON YOUR MIND WAS JUST IMPORTANT & WORTHY THAN WHAT I HAD DISCUSSED WITH ████████████. SIS I LOVE YOU EQUALLY NO MORE NO LESS THAN I DO GRAMS, MOMS, AND ██████ I SWARE YA'LL MY EVERYTHANG. SIS I KNOW YOUR OF AGE WHERE YOU CAN TAKE CARE OF YOURSELF BUT IT'Z A BROTHERS INSTICTS TO BE CONCERNED ABOUT YOU THAT'S WHY I ASKED WHO HOUSE YOU WERE GOING TO AFTER THE VISIT I'M GOING TO STAY IN YOUR BUSINESS LONG AS IM BREATHING SO GET USE TO IT ☺. SIS IM PROUD TO SEE YOU KEEPING YOSELF TOGETHER PHYSICALLY, MENTALLY YOUR STILL GRINDING WHICH I RESPECT TO FULLEST BECAUSE STUDYING IS STRAIGHT DISCIPLINE — THE PAYOFF GONE BE WORTH IT — SIS I HEARD OH BOY YOU LIKE IS ABOUT TO COME HOME AND IM SURE YOUR UNDER PRESSURE TO MAKE A DECISION (SEXUALLY). I CAN'T CALL THAT DUE TO IT'S ON YOU TO DECIDE WHO'S WORTH RECEIVING SOMETHING SO SACRET & PRECIOUS. I KNOW ONE THING ONCE YOU GIVE IT UP DO YOU THINK YA'LL BE CLOSER, WILL HE TREAT YOU BETTER, WILL YOU BE HAPPIER? TAKE ALL THOSE QUESTIONS INTO CONSIDERA-

ION BEFORE REACTING. [redacted]. SHEEDA
IM A BIT MORE HARDER ON BOYS YALL MESS WITH I
KNOW HOW YOU THINK [redacted] SO IM GOING TO ALWAYS ANALYZE THINGS
IN DEPTH. SIS YOUR LOOKING CUTER AS YOU AGE SO
THE MEN GO FLOCK BUT LONG AS YOU STAY AHEAD
OF THE GAME PEOPLE PLAY IN THIS WICKET WORLD
YOU'LL BE ALRIGHT. SIS DON'T BE SO QUICK TO
INVOLVE YOUR EMOTIONS INTO RELATIONSHIPS IF THINGS
DON'T WORK OUT IT WON'T BE NO LOSS ON YOUR END.
IF YOU KEEP IT NO STRINGS ATTACHED THEN YOUR
EXPECTATIONS WON'T BE THAT HIGH "YOU FIGG ME?" WHAT
I LOOK LIKE LETTING MY LIL SIS BECOME A VICTIM
OF THE HANDS OF ANDNISSA [redacted] ITZ MY DUTY
TO LACE YOUR BOOTS ON ALL WALKS OF LIFE EVEN
THOUGH I KANT HOLD YOUR HAND THROUGH THE JOURNEY
RASHEEDA YOU'VE BEEN SLACKING AS WELL ON GETTING
AT ME ABOUT WHATEVER SO ITS BEEN HARD FOR A
GENIUS TO ASSIST YOU WHEN IM LEFT WITH LITTLE
TO GO ON. SIS WATCH OVER MOMS, GRAMS, AUNTY, AND
OF COURSE THE YOUNG TROPIKALS [redacted]..
I LOVE YOU AND MISS YOU ALREADY GOD'S MY WITNESS
I FEEL LIKE IM BEING CHEATED NOT BEING ABLE TO
BE IN YALL COMPANY I PRAY IN DUE TIME GOD
WILL FREE ME AND THROW HIS SON BACK INTO
YA'LL PRESENCE. UNTIL THEN STAY FOCUSED SIS—

The letters kept us busy. They kept us up to date. They gave us something to look forward to. In a way, I didn't have to confide in friends at the time who'd probably play telephone with my business, I was able to send it to my brother who appeared not to judge. He may have thought I had a couple of screws loose depending on the day I wrote the letter, but never placed judgment on any of my decisions.

I am sure that my antics and character kept him going on days, he was able to be someone for me although he wasn't physically present. In every letter he wrote back he made sure to provide perspective from the outside looking in, some motivation, inspiration, and truth – real raw and uncut. I respected him for that. I loved him for that.

All the love, attention, and energy that I would've put into a relationship, I was pouring into our relationship, one that I knew would surely last all my days. This, I was sure.

MOE

Regardless of my behavior in prison, or whether I'd been in the SHU or not, my sister Rasheeda made it a priority to write, visit, and love me unconditionally. She became a regular visitor, often traveling hours to different prisons and sacrificing her youthful time to come chill with her big brother. Her maturity came fast, and her intellect followed suit. During our visits we would discuss family matters, relationships, school, career choices, etc. As time would proceed we'd discuss world politics, race, racial conflicts, apartheid, law, and general life issues.

My little sister made it easy to think about her safety because she's not the girl who's into hanging in the streets, clubbing, fighting, gossiping, or going from dude to dude (besides the crushes she would wreck my nerves talking about). We've made an unspoken vow to never introduce each other's mate until we know it's official. I'm old school in the sense that my sister and daughter are gems, so I have high expectations on who they date. I am overly protective, so my understanding is narrow, and my love is just that deep.

My sister keeps me grounded and balanced, always speaking in a humble and harmonious voice while directing our attention, energy, and dialogue on productive goals. These years have been agonizing due to how much pain has rained down on us as a family. Without each other's love, strengths, and loyalty I'm certain the result would have been much more severe.

I'd been sent to California's farthest and most violent prison at the time, "Pelican Bay." Pelican Bay is an 11-hour drive from my hometown of Los Angeles. This prison is close to the state of Oregon. It's a dangerous ride. You sometimes have to drive around mountains, at times in bad weather, in the middle of nowhere. The inmate population in Pelican Bay had been deemed the worst prison, partly due to inmates hardly ever receiving visitors. It's similar to being on an abandoned island. The inmates call Pelican Bay "lose your b*tch island."

In weathering my own storm, my own blessing had come. My daughter's mother came back into my life which was cool. She'd been my first love and our history had been off and on. Still I'd never turned my back on her based on the fact she'd given me something that's priceless (my daughter). Upon reuniting, my baby mama was willing to make the sacrifice; she brought my siblings, grams, and daughter up there to visit me.

I remember my grams saying "Moe, I love you, but I'll never come back up here." She complained about the long ride. Grams would complain about my daughter's mom driving too fast and said, "She had the nerve to speak about me smoking a pack of cigarettes during the agonizing ride."

I laughed but felt guilty for putting my loved ones through that hardship. At the time my plan was to stay active in whatever capacity I could. I was sure they'd get tired of me and get me transferred to a closer prison. Well, I was ten years in and around this time I had lost my granny, paw paw, and a myriad of close homies. In the underworld (streets) death is always around the corner.

My world became a nightmare with the tragic news that continued to pile on up. It seemed like there was always something. I remember specifically one of the chaplain's calls that hit home and hurt deeply. The chaplain got word to me that my younger relative Ramone was killed at the age of 25. At the age of 17 I had decided to get teardrops tattooed on my face, symbolizing never ending tears. After so many deaths and killings of people I loved, I became numb to it and honestly the tears dried up.

But losing Ramone broke the flood gate. I watched him grow up and admired almost everything about him; his personality, his style, and the love we had for each other as men in our family. Losing him was different because he was young and had so much life to live. I also knew what losing him meant for my aunt who raised me, and the hurt it caused to our family. Unfortunately, before I could begin to grieve his loss, exactly three years later his older brother Derek was killed at the age of 32. Now, Derek was special to me so my feelings towards our loss of him I'll keep close. However, they are both always with me, always.

For me to be subjected to a plantation with chains, shackles, and a zoo-like environment, it became first nature to have a turnt up attitude and built-in aggression. My violent mentality at that time kept me slammed. My motto had been if you were on the line (actively amongst the general population) longer than 6 months without getting active, in my eyes you were inactive.

These long durations of being housed in a small cage unknowingly brought the growth I needed to elevate both mentally and spiritually. When you're housed in the hole (removed from the general population for disciplinary reasons) your privileges become limited. You're allowed (1) appliance. In contrast to the mainline, the hole can be unbearable, unless you adjust by soul-searching, studying, physically exercising, writing, and finding the good in yourself to counteract this inhumane circumstance. Experiencing my own coldest winter ever, I was blessed nevertheless that my homies, my home girls, my female friends, and my family held me down. The calendar marked ten years in prison, and I was still remembered.

Now I had somebody who was beginning to stand out, shine bright, and lead the march in this conquest to one day free myself physically and psychologically – my sister. My daughter, grams, aunt, and mom's nurturing talks with me had a way of breaking the chains, the cycle I'd inherited, and the negative thought process that I was battling. I would like to extend my appreciation to them because it was needed, required, and mandatory to feel loved, desired, and supported in a place like this grave called prison if I was in this fight for my freedom.

"Dear Diary,
I just want to be free."

DED: When Thugz Cry (TUPAC)

Sept 8, 2007

Sis what it does loveone? Hopefully this missive comes at a time when you are focused, and you find serenity in my choice of words. Sis it's been hella long since you've opened and shared yo inner thoughts with me. I didn't trip because I had to accept, you're entering that maturity course where privacy is must so I gave you your space 111 feet. I really anticipated a visit from you because it's indeed a lot that needs to be discussed and addressed.

Sis, I am so proud of you for many reasons. It's no limit to the potential you possess and I'm glad you're not being distracted by nothing senseless that will stop you from succeeding your goals. I respect your grind and sis fasho the pay off gone be worth this time, energy, and sacrificing (Education is key).

Sis I am sure you and moms know I'm back hell bound (hole) within a cage. Yea I'll be out of sight for a while on this trip due to the police warned if I get caught up for anything else I'd be labeled a program failure which would result in me doing years hole time. I'll be sending the bulk of my property home to you accept my TV. I can keep that when I get to the manhole (Shu). Keep my flicks in the kut because I'll need for you to send them back to me when I get settled.

NE ways you will be receiving alot of mail from me for you and ████ ████████. Sis I know you be busy and like I said I support and respect the grind you on but your big brah needs you and I am limited on the people I can actually depend on.

Sis, I love you more than you may realize. I basically feel like your equal to how I view my daughter ██████ (In a fatherly protective way).

It's no need for me to ever preach to you since you are on your game ahead of your peers in a league of your own "that's the business"!

Sheeda tell your twin I said what's up with them flicks he was supposed to send? Tell blood b- safe, shake them sukas and get money! I wrote ████ explaining that I need some stamp envelopes and a few dollars on my books. See what's up with that. I Love you sis and miss yall to death. As time passes, pictures fades, niggas turn fake, but my love for yall remains strong.

Kisses and hugs - "In the everlasting struggling. Figg moe"

- -

DED: WHEN THUGS KRY.. (TUPAC)

SEP 8, 07—

SIS WHAT it DOES LOVEONE? HOPEFULLY THIS MISSIVE COMES AT A TIME WHEN YOUR FOCUSED AND YOU FIND SERENITY IN MY CHOICE OF WORDS. SIS ITS BEEN HELLA LONG SINCE YOU'VE OPENED UP AND SHARED YO INNER THOUGHTS WITH ME. I DIDN'T TRIP BECAUSE I HAD TO ACCEPT YOU'RE ENTERING THAT MATURITY COURSE WHERE PRIVACY IS A MUST SO I GAVE YOU SPACE 1 1 1 FEET. I REALLY ANTICIPATED A VISIT FROM YOU BECAUSE ITS INDEED ALOT THAT NEEDS TO BE DISCUSSED & ADDRESSED. SIS IM SO PROUD OF YOU FOR SO MANY REASONS IT'S NO LIMITS TO THE POTENTIAL YOU POSSESS AND IM GLAD YOUR NOT BEING DESTRACTED BY NOTHING SENSELESS THAT'LL STOP YOU FROM SUCCEEDING YOUR GOALS— I RESPECT YOUR GRIND AND SIS FASHOW THE PAYOFF GONE BE WORTH THIS TIME, ENERGY, & SACRIFICING. (EDUCATION IS KEY)

SIS AS IM SURE YOU AND MOMS KNOW IM BACK HELLBOUND (HOLE) A CAGE WITHIN A CAGE. YEAH I'LL BE OUT OF SIGHT FOR A WHILE THIS TRIP DUE TO THE POLICE WARNED IF I GOT CAUGHT UP FOR ANYTHING ELSE I'D BE LABELED A PROGRAM FAILURE WHICH WOULD RESULT IN ME DOING YEARS HOLE TIME. I'LL BE SENDING THIS →

bulk of my property home to you accept my T.V. I can keep that when I get to the mainhole (SHU). Keep my flicks in the kut because I'll need for you to send them back when I get settled..

Neways you'll be receiving alot of mail from me for you & [redacted] sis I know you be busy and like I said I support & respect the grind you on but ya big bram needs you and im limited on people I can actually depend on. Sis I love you more than you may realize I basically feel like your equal to how I view [redacted] (in a fatherly protective way) It's no need for me to ever preach to you since you on your game ahead of your peers in a league of your own! That's the bizness! — Sheeda tell to twin I said what's up with them flicks he was suppose to send? Tell blood to b-safe and shake them suckas and get money! I wrote [redacted] explaining that I need some stamp envalopes & a few dollars on my books. Seek whats ↑? I love you sis and miss all ya'll to death as time passes pictures fade, females fade, niggas turn fake, but my love for y'all remains - strong - kisses & hugs — "In the everlasting struggle Figgmoe!"

CHAPTER 3:
TRUST NO MAN

RASHEEDA

For so long I had been writing, visiting, and being a good little sister because it was something that I was accustomed to. "You are there for your family no matter what" was the constant voice that would always ring in my mind. A part of me was there for my brother because I wanted to, but also because it was something that I learned early on I was supposed to do. Grams did it for her husband. Then, for my parents. My mommy did it for my daddy, and here I was doing it for my brothers. Did I love my brother? Absolutely. I loved everything about him but as I grew older, I started to notice that as I was maturing our familial bond was not as strong as I desired it to be.

Yes, no question that I loved him. Mommy taught us to love thy brother and as I matured, I remember how much I had admired him. I admired him and the other men in my family because of the way they provided, protected, and always made me feel safe when they were around. Nonetheless, time and distance have their way of getting in the way of things. We know that to be true in any relationship, whether you experience a long-distance relationship or are away from your loved one for a long period of time. Time can break a bond if you let it. Space, distance, time, and all the barriers in between had its way of creating so much separation. For a minute I lost a sense of connection as I grew into a young lady. The love I had for my brother was there but there was a disconnect for a short period of time (well at least for me).

My brother's visits started to decrease because life was happening for everyone. Environmental stressors, inability to take off work, and a host of other factors got in the way of completing my regular trips up north. Not only that but for a while my brother was subjected to long terms in the SHU which made it impossible to maintain communication. The relationship for me suffered. I started to question my role as a sister and ask myself, "Would I be a bad sister if I stopped writing?"

How long would I have to be subjected to 3-way calls, gathering information for custom boxes and CD's, or finding a location that could take money for J Pay? It was something I was used to from obligation. This was my brother, and I was going to be loyal to his program. Again, mommy raised us this way.

What did I know about loyalty? What did loyalty even mean? I just knew I was becoming tired of running a program that none of my friends seemed to understand. The outside world would never understand! At least I thought they wouldn't.

I was 18 or 19 years of age if I recall correctly, when I became familiar with the word *loyalty* for the first time.

I met a good friend in high school who later became my best friend. We talked about everything. He kept my secrets safe and if I had ever needed to feel joy 'just because', he was the first person I would contact. I knew he would bring a smile out of me that was deeply rooted in love, authenticity, and bliss. This best friend of mine introduced me to the word loyalty. I swear I felt like that was his most used and favorite word.

"Loyalty this, loyalty that." He ate, slept, and moved demonstrating and speaking of nothing more than love and loyalty. "Imani you loyal", "Jones, stay loyal" he would say to me. He often called me by my middle name and last name. He only would call me Rasheeda if I made him upset. "Jones, loyalty is not a word. It's a lifestyle." I mean everything he did resulted in some form of loyal action. Therefore, it was imperative that I knew what it meant to be "loyal."

I would itch every time he mentioned the word, curious to ask, "Best friend what does it mean to be loyal?"

At that age you'd think I would know. I didn't. Everyone thought I was so smart and held me in so much regard that my ego wouldn't dare allow me to fix my mouth and ask what he meant. So, I never did. Each time he said it I just went along with it. "Yea I'm loyal! Yep!"

Given the amount of love I had for him, I trusted that he would never call me something I wasn't. He loved me like that. I trusted him so whenever he described me, I knew it was a good trait and characteristic to have and so I was cool with it. From that day I believed him to be true, I was loyal.

In the time I was introduced to this concept with no full understanding, my best friend's legacy was interrupted. He died from an unfortunate motorcycle accident. I still mourn his loss to this day. Before his demise I never got an understanding from him, but I would soon find out. Loyalty was something that I was determined to know more about so that I could represent and carry my best friend's memory forever.

Coincidently, the same year of my friend's passing I returned to my full-time job as a security officer. The irony of me being in a position of anything remotely close to law enforcement having seen all the pain it caused was crazy. But it was what it was. I was a security officer, and my job was to observe, report, and benefit from how easy this job was, in order to further my own personal goals of advancing my education. With that said, I was the best security guard ever with the most convenient station. I literally got paid to say, "goodnight and have a great weekend", smile, and find ways to educate myself more.

Honestly, I looked for almost anything to pass 8 hours of my day 4 days a week. I wasn't big on reading just yet. I mean as a kid *Ramona, Junie B. Jones* and other kid friendly novels would have my attention but that love somehow disappeared. My life was nothing compared to Ramona whose stressors weren't like mine. Thinking back, I wasn't big on a lot of things after graduating high school (sorry, I had a moment there).

One thing I have come to learn is that you must be open to the possibility of being introduced to things, and you may begin to find interest. As much as I once enjoyed reading, I didn't regain a liking for it until I worked there.

A coworker of mine, an older Black woman, found interest in developing a co-worker relationship with me, and to my advantage she loved to read. Hood novels were her thing, and there's no shade to that. After every read she would walk over to my workstation in the last hour of her shift and start talking about them. The hood novels ranged in different topics. The topics went from drug stories, baby mama drama, betrayal, and more. You name the type of story and there was a book waiting for you to read, ready to convey how the Black struggle can be beautiful and cold at the same time. Real, yet full of entertainment.

Trust No Man was the first book she suggested and the second hood novel that I'd read. *Trust No Man* by Cash was a book trilogy that was themed around "loyalty to those who are loyal." The author started writing fiction stories to cope through his circumstances. The author was incarcerated serving more than 22 years in prison, striving to teach and entertain others through his paper and pen.

This book not only caught my attention because of the author and his ability to create regardless of his circumstance, but I was also able to gather an in-depth understanding of what it meant to be loyal! Yes! I don't know if you've ever been intrigued by something and once you got an in-depth understanding, felt like you had just gained access to that world and are no longer an outsider looking in. Well, that's how I felt when I read this book. I had watched movies, heard stories, etc. about what it meant to live a life of loyalty. Learning about the word loyalty from my best friend and then experiencing it in this book, made me feel it. The examples in the book provided me concrete examples of what it truly meant.

Loyal – giving or showing firm and consistent support or allegiance to a person. Due to my overexcitement, I thought and felt this book would re-connect my brother Omar and I. I was beyond excited to purchase the trilogy collection and have it shipped off to him for dialogue. You see my dad was a scholar and the love for education and seeking knowledge was something his children picked up on early. I knew reading was something my brother enjoyed. I couldn't wait for him to receive his package, read his new reads, and develop something we could both share. I was looking for anything to stay connected to him and this was my first attempt at doing so.

"Hey sis. I got your package in the mail. Thanks for the book."

I knew he would enjoy the book and be entertained based on his reaction after the first series. We went back and forth for a while on our favorite parts, what parts stood out, and what lessons we learned. I swear reading that book made me feel like I was ready to take on all the worries of the world for my brother. It also provided me with insight with how cold and heartless the streets could be.

My brother teased me a lot. Always calling me a 'square' and naïve to the Los Angeles streets. I would always whine back and tell him how knowledgeable I was. In all honesty I had no clue. I had to study books, listen to music, and watch TV shows to feel connected when I was living it. Drug life, friends being murdered, injustice, betrayal, drama, and trauma – I was dead smack in the center of it and didn't even know. I guess the family did a good job because I was sheltered a great deal.

Trust No Man series one was good, two was good, and by the third one I guess we had run our course with the book. I'd be lying if I said I wasn't sad. The book was the only thing that I felt made us close, because we both shared a common interest. Nonetheless, I had to respect his wishes. My brother shared that he was over reading hood novels. He said it did nothing for his spirit or mind and was pure entertainment, but entertainment to a life that he had lived and that stirred so many emotions. He was reading a fiction story but his life at such a young age was far more complex than any book could talk about, and I didn't understand it.

"So, what are we going to do now?" I would ask, looking for the next best thing to keep us connected.

"Sis, send me some sh*t I can learn from. That's going to expand my thinking, my position, my growth, my life."

Ummmmm, for a minute I was stuck but he was asking for something that was worthwhile. I guess I'd never really thought to tap into that side of him, or was even at the point in my life where I could introduce it to him. I wasn't well-read, well-traveled, well-anything. I was just a young girl trying to keep her sanity from all that life had brought me thus far.

I felt scared that we wouldn't be able to connect. However, it was the perfect time. I admired his mind, and respected his thoughts and opinions so much. It only motivated me and sparked an interest to search for some stuff I had never done. I was down to change the narrative. I was down to start a relationship being connected by something more than just my old feelings of obligation. With this new request of his, our connection would introduce me to a world I had been dying to explore for a long time. In this space I was not only able to discover that I had been displaying loyalty this whole time, but that I was ready to seek knowledge in literature, places, and people and become smarter, wiser, and better with my brother's support along the way.

- -

June 8, 2009

-Sis, Hi my queen. It's been a minute since we've communicated so when your missive arrived I was delighted and anxious to see how you have been living the college life. I sent a brief letter and a prison-mart card, did you receive it? It's been so long since you wrote, I figured you adopted another elder brother :). N.E.Ways, hearing from you brought me a much needed smile and after reading your letter (peace/healing) was put into motion concerning my soul.

Sis, it's hard on my end. I'm fighting a psychological warfare and trying to keep my temperament in check, which has been difficult to sustain since I'm in defensive mode. You know I was anticipating being released from this shu in May, but as you heard they concocted up lies to retain me back here, so I'm singing the blues. I'm praying moms and other advocates call up here speaking on my behalf about this unjust investigation and solitary confinement. My mail, my pictures, etc, are all being withheld. All my prior visitors are being disapproved, it seems as if I can't win—!

Sis, I am glad you recognize when you slack, and have that willpower to bounce back (in general) on every aspect. I'll call it self-discipline, a resilience to succeed and be self-sufficient. I love you sis and respect your drive. Continue to climb those mountains until you reach the top. I believe in my baby sis and trust you will achieve your goals, so focus girl!

That's bool yall went to go visit Lee. Did yall take any flicks? [redacted] Aunty and I have been corresponding as of late, I'm trying to fill any voids she may have emotionally. We've basically leaned on each other for strength while enduring grief over our losses. She said it looks good for Lee's future concerning his freedom, so that is a sign of better days for us as a whole.

Sis continues to watch over The Tropikals, [redacted], [redacted], and [redacted]. It's going to be times when you feel annoyed, infuriated, or unappreciated but remember you're just doing what's needed to guide them in a lady like fashion. We all appreciate your positive presence. Believe me sis we speak your name with admiration. Sis, I've tried to open up a line of communication with your twin but I received no feedback, which is something I am not use to. MM dont do the swanging. I love him and care about his safety, since I am certain he is ill advised out there in them streets, "but what am I to do?" Let me know sis because he is worth saving/caring about. We're all we have. Tell mommy I love her and I pray she get back on her feet "financially." We don't need any extra stress. Sis, when you give moms, aunty, and grams a shout out for their upcoming b-days send mind as well. Well Angel, this is the part I hate, saying goodbyes. But I must drop the ink for now.

You mean so much to me "If this world were mine" I'd give you diamonds, pearls, & furs. You're a queen and deserve to be treated like one. That's my mission. —You take care of yourself and don't delay your brother that long again. — I love you :)

- -

June 8, 09—

Sis, Hi my queen. It's been a minute since we've communicated so when your missive arrived I was delighted and anxious to see how you've been living the college life. I sent a brief letter and a prison-mart B'day card, did you receive it? It's been so long since you wrote, I figured you adopted another elder brother ☺. Anyways, hearing from you brought me a much needed smile and after reading your letter (peace/healing) was put into motion concerning my soul. Sis it's hard on my end, im fighting a psychological warfare and trying to keep my temperment in check, which has been difficult to sustain since im in defensive mode. You know I was anticipating being released from this SHU in May, but as you've heard they've concocted up lies to retain me back here, so im singing the blues. I'm praying moms and other advocates call up here speaking on my behalf about this unjust investigation & solitary confinement. My mail, pictures, etc are being withheld. All my prior visitors are being disapproved, it seems as if I can't win—! Sis im glad you recognize when you slack, and have that will-power to bounce back (in general) on every aspect. I'll call it self-disciple, a resilience to succeed and be self-sufficient. I love you sis and so respect your drive, continue to climb them mountains until you reach the top. I believe in my baby sis and trust you'll achieve your goals, so focus girl! Thats bool yall went to visit Lee. Did

Y'ALL TAKE ANY FLICKS? █████ AND I HAVE BEEN CORRESPONDING OF LATE, I'M TRYING TO FILL ANY VOIDS SHE MAY HAVE EMOTIONALLY. WE'VE BASICALLY LEANED ON EACHOTHER FOR STRENGTH WHILE ENDURING GRIEF OVER OUR LOSSES. SHE SAID IT'S LOOKING GOOD FOR LEE'S FUTURE CONCERNING HIS FREEDOM, SO THATS A SIGN OF BETTER DAYS FOR US AS A WHOLE.

SIS CONTINUE TO WATCH OVER █████, █████, AND █████. IT'S GOING TO BE THEM TIMES WHEN YOU FEEL ANNOYED, INFURIATED, OR UNAPPRECIATED BUT REMEMBER YOU'RE JUST DOING WHAT'S NEEDED TO GUIDE THEM IN A LADYLIKE FASHION. WE ALL APPRECIATE YOUR POSITIVE PRESENCE. BELIEVE ME SIS WE SPEAK YOUR NAME WITH HIGH ADMIRATION. SIS I'VE TRIED TO OPEN UP A LINE OF COMMUNICATION WITH YOUR TWIN BUT I RECEIVED NO FEED BACK, WHICH IS SOMETHING I'M NOT USE TOO. MEM DON'T DO THE SWANGING. I LOVE HIM AND CARE ABOUT HIS SAFETY, SINCE I'M CERTAIN HE'S ILL-ADVISED OUT THERE IN THEM STREETS, BUT "WHAT AM I TO DO?" LET ME KNOW SIS BECAUSE HE'S WORTH SAVING/CARING ABOUT. WE'RE ALL WE HAVE. TELL MOMMY I LOVE HER AND I PRAY SHE GET BACK ON HER FEET "FINACIALLY". WE DON'T NEED ANY EXTRA STRESS. SIS WHEN YOU GIVE MOMS, AUNTY, AND GRAMS A SHOUT OUT FOR THEIR UPCOMING B'DAY'S ~ SEND MINES AS WELL. WELL ANGEL, THIS IS THE PART I HATE, SAYING GOODBYES BUT I MUST DROP THE INK FOR NOW. YOU MEAN SO MUCH TO ME "IF THIS WORLD WERE MINE" I'D GIVE YOU DIAMONDS, PEARLS, & FURS, YOUR A QUEEN AND DESERVES TO BE TREATED LIKE ONE. THATS MY MISSION ~ YOU TAKE CARE OF YOURSELF AND DON'T DELAY YOUR BROTHER THAT LONG AGAIN – I LOVE U :)

MOE

As my world shifted, my personal hunger turned to higher learning; educating myself on a broader scale was the desire I had developed to sharpen my mind, which I knew would create a change in me. To my delight Rasheeda had blossomed into a positive force mentally. She'd been accepted into college, which was rewarding, and a proud and prideful moment for our family and community.

Now that she'd developed into a beautiful and intellectual young woman, our conversations got interesting. We still spent limited time talking about her relationships with guy friends, based on my overprotective state and wanting to shield my bloodline. If it were up to me, she'd be a nun or forever a virgin. In my eyes my sister was an angel, so innocent and worthy of a gentleman who'd naturally be willing to go above and beyond to protect, respect, cherish and provide for her. The young man would have to get interviewed by me if he thought he'd ever get a clearance into our circle. (Sister, I sincerely apologize that I couldn't be there for you during your turmoil with love your first time around).

We started opening up about grim realities like prison politics, gangs, drugs, ghetto activities, and common hood gossip. My sis was the first female birthed to an all-male family outside of my moms, aunty, and grams so she was right there amidst the ghetto hardships. She knew all my homies, both dead and alive. She grew up with my little bro, her twin, and a generation of neighborhood friends. Even as my little sister attended hood functions, she dealt with it very minimally and from afar. I don't think she fully understood the rawness of the streets.

My sis always shunned the gang lifestyle. While she hadn't been interested in it personally, she embraced a part of its culture due to her brothers, cousins, and uncles' heavy affiliation. On our visits we'd sometimes laugh about different rumors or even have slight disagreements about her talking to someone who I felt would breach our family security. It has always been my duty to teach my sis, daughter, and female relatives with certain things based on the myriad of potential threats. My sis can sometimes be naïve to the game so I put extra security over her moves whenever I could.

For the most part our relationship is cool. I trust in her decision-making skills and ability. As my little sister matured, she was compelled to find her own identity. I have watched her grow and made note that she refuses to become another statistic or stereotype. On most visits we would continue dialogue about stimulating our brains to become better individuals; people who weren't content with the whirlwind of bullsh*t historically done to our people. After a much needed talk I noticed that her mind became sharper. We suggested books that we knew could enhance, support, and hold space for our common goals, common plights, common pain, common sense, and common interests. Together, we've championed a bond that this distance, barbed wire facility, and oppressive system can't break.

I think she told you but let me tell you too. She sent an urban novel to me and our younger brother who was incarcerated as well – *Trust No Man*. I was active in the prison but at this point in my life I yearned for something deeper; in my spirit, I wasn't interested in fiction books. It was no longer entertaining to me. My soul thirsted for an outlet to flush the demons that existed internally within me, and certain books fulfilled that obligation.

Books are informative; the right information received and processed can produce insight, understanding, growth, and mental fortitude. And even though I wanted more thought-provoking books, I also wanted to bond with my siblings regardless of how we did it. We all read *Trust No Man* and even imported a theme to our three-way bond. After all was said and done, we formed a theme from the book – love is love but loyalty is everything." The words went hand and hand with what we stood for and displayed in our integrity and character daily.

My sister was wet behind the ears, and I laugh as I think about it. She was without knowledge of certain lifestyles, so this urban novel had her open, curious, and eager to send and read more. She was right, the series did create a light topic to discuss and laugh about during our many conversations. But again, I know we all needed more. I started to suggest non-fiction books. It was now my time to shine and show what was in my literacy library.

The things you don't get to see often is that although I was active, I was also smart and well-read. One of my favorite suggested readings was *The New Jim Crow* by Michelle Alexander. This reading gave light to my complaints and bitterness, and solutions to the abstract of the inhumane conditions we're faced with even in this present day.

It used to infuriate me when my sister would tell me how she had to wait in the long visiting line only to finally reach the entry point and still get turned around over what the hell she had on. They'd often send her back two or three times to change, never satisfied. The treatment that she endured is just like the treatment of so many. It is malpractice, often negatively affecting the inmates mentally because he is being denied his full visiting time and rights. The visitor can sometimes become so enraged with this run around that they lose their patience and leave. The saga and drama with my sister's visiting stories pissed me off plenty of times. Rasheeda has often had to calm me down after notifying me about the prison staff's foul treatment and behavior.

I think that is what I respect and love most about her. Even in my worst moments and darkest hours, she often found the strength and focus needed to calm me down. She has never allowed prison placement, the visiting strife, or my bipolar negative ass impede her from being by my side.

For the readers who are not familiar with the experience of visiting prisons let me fill you in. It is a mental, emotional, and financial sacrifice on the sacrificer. It is costly in terms of gas, a rental car, hotel room stay, food, etc. Also, it's a long drive and can be dangerous if one is sleep deprived. Sadly, I have met friends during my fight for freedom who have lost kids, wives, and family due to them falling asleep while driving.

Imagine having to live life in a grave called prison with a daily conscious of not having the ones you loved here any longer because they lost their lives trying to visit you. So, I am always prayed up, on edge, and then blessed knowing my folks made it here and back home safely. These visits, our talks, nor our time together can amount to our family being separated during this ordeal. But my sister's presence has given me the tools needed to think positively and helped me experience being loved, while still learning how to remain hopeful.

Rasheeda has been a ride or die in my evolution. Our time is often spent talking about productivity. She won't accept me venturing off in muddy waters too long, it feels like she has a two-minute limit. She'll give me a stern look, as if to say, "okay change the subject", often redirecting and shifting the energy.

"What's up Mr. Jones," she'd say to get me back on track. Even though I'm naturally stubborn, I'm not ignorant so it is always an easy call and just like that we shift gears.

Thankfully, we've never experienced a fallout. We respectfully agree to disagree but attitudes, cursing, or expressing any sentiments of disrespect to each other are unacceptable and off limits. In the following chapter, I'll discuss our mother Hen who I credit for instilling our ethics. Without respect, honor, and love you have limited appreciation and integrity. Value is defined as being worthy of genuine love, and sacrifice for my brothers and sisters.

8.22.10 To: Sheeda Fr: Mr. Understood

Sis, what it do queen? Hopefully, your copacetic and maintaining a positive mind, body & soul. I love & miss yall! Now to the business: I received your missive and was charmed/excited to hear from my dear sista. Sheeda my intention is to always change the mindset when I strike you for the betterment concerning us as a family. Shit, when you shine, rise, fall or hurt. I'm affected. Your actions will always create a reaction from me, that's how much we are spiritually connected. N'e ways it's good to know you received something knowledgeable while chilling in Fresno, instead of us just seeing what is in front of you. You are still soul searching for what brings you joy internally. I hope you have some cool times as well chilling with oh boy. Life is a balancing act. Sis I am back in the hole. [redacted].

Sis, on "moms" I'm hella bitter, I found out I never had a lawyer. All these years I am under the assumption I am being fought for by a legal appellate but in all actuality, I'm being lied to and (deceived) by my own. Hell yea I'm salty, hurt, and disappointed. It's like my life (freedom) aint worthy of attention, support, or time consumption. Don't speak on this to anyone based on it's no purpose. I don't need any excuse or sob letters as to why things are the way they are. I'll continue to write you long letters given all of me (mentally) it is my duty. But others will receive formal kites if that. Sis I got to make up for the years lost of not pushing for freedom. I've been writing to legal offices seeking aid as of late. Pops even has been a supporter in this push so the fight isn't over, it's just begun!

Sis, I really feel you can be vital in me pursuing a lot of needs especially, with us utilizing our minds, resources, and technology (Facebook). I've been going nuts trying to find someone I can turn to for simple shit such as putting a site together for me. You have the means, my flicks, prison address, my bio, etc.

8.22.10 ~

To: Sheeda Fr: MrMisunderstood

Sis, what it do queen? Hopefully your copeacetic and maintaining a positive mind & body. I love & miss y'all! Now to the business: I received your missive and was charmed/excited to hear from my dear sista. Sheeda my intentions is to always change the mindset when I strike you for the imbetterment concerning us as a family. Shit when u shine, rise, fall, or hurt, im affected. Your actions will always create a reaction from me, thats how much we're spiritually connected. N.E.ways it's good to know you received something knowledgable while chilling in Fresno, instead of just seeing whats in front of you, you're now soul searching for what brings you joy internally. I hope you had some cool times as well chilling with oh boy. Life is a balancing act. Sis im back in the hole. ... on "moms" im hella bitter, I found out I never had a lawyer, all these years im under thee assumption im being fought for by a legal appellant but in all actuality im being lied too (deceived) by my own. Hell yeah im salty, hurt, and disappointed. It's like my life (freedom) ain't worthy of attention, support, & time consumption. Don't speak on this to anyone based on it's no purpose I don't need and excuses or sob letters for why things are the way they are. I'll continue to write you long letters given all of me (mentally) it's my duty. But others will receive formal kites if that. Sis I got to make up for the years lost of not pushing for freedom. I've been writing legal offices seeking aid of late. Pops even has been a supporter in this push so the fight isn't over, it's just began!! Sis I really feel you can be vital in my pursuing alot of needs especially with us utilizing our minds, resources, and technology (website facebook). I've been going nuts trying to find someone I can turn too for simple shit such as putting a site together for me. You have the means; my flicks, prison address, my bio, e.t.c. Niggas in here getting hella mail from white hoes in Alaska old, married, but swangin dollars. Sis I'm thinking bigga freedom, $, (support). I just got a kite from Louie and I →

CHAPTER 4:
KEYS TO THE CITY

RASHEEDA

My heart was heavy when leaving the city of LA. It was a love-hate relationship that I had with my native land. As much as I loved it here, I hated it too. I never really felt safe, secure, or felt I had any purpose if I wasn't in the company of my family. My routine would consist of working, going to school, spending time with my boyfriend and that was it. Oh and of course visiting my brothers, niece, and friends in different prisons throughout California.

I had no identity. I always found myself being identified as "such and such's little sister" or "such and such's twin, aunty, or girlfriend." Never just me for me. I felt I had no sense of direction, purpose, or anything unique about me despite what my family thought of me; I didn't know my "why."

For a while I was ok with that. I made enough money where I could buy things that satisfied my needs. I was a simple girl and didn't ask for much. Hair, nails, and a cute outfit from Forever 21 or a real sleek and fashionable outfit from a boutique in LA called Nobody Jones. I was able to purchase my first car and live comfortably rent-free. Just my mom and me. Not to mention I had one of the best boyfriends in the world at this time, I'll call him "Superman."

Superman came at the perfect time in my life. He was the next relationship I had after "my love" and I knew my brothers would immediately approve. He had no gang affiliations (if a person is affiliated with anything that is important in LA). He was strong, smart, had an outgoing personality, wise, well mannered, a gentle man, loving, charismatic, charming, talented, had leadership qualities, educated, a family man, and had a smile that lit every room he entered.

With all that Superman had to offer, he also made sure that he offered me a commitment and a promise to love me, all of me. The broken parts of me, the sacred parts of me, the insecure parts of me. He worked overtime to make sure he was patient with me and kind. We meshed well together. I can count on my hands the number of times we argued, because we never had much to argue about. I pushed him to be better and he surely did the same for me. He didn't like how spoiled I was or how much of a brat I would become when I didn't get my way, but he contributed to much of that in me.

He'd buy me flowers just because on Wednesday, and wouldn't mind waking up late at night to fry us fish and potatoes or donuts. He made sure my car stayed in maintenance, that I was doing well in work and school, and that every opportunity he had to create those memorable and fairytale moments for me, he would.

He knew I'd always believed in fairytales. I thank him for always making me feel like a princess.

I did not cook or clean and hadn't develop any domestic traits just yet. Growing up we never had space to fulfill that obligation, our mommy made sure those roles were covered. So, I got away a lot of the time with being a cute, loving, and supportive girlfriend and that was enough. At least I thought it was enough. Most days it was.

Superman came into my life to show me how I was supposed to be treated. I no longer had any male figures in my life (physically present) so he was what I knew and was leaning on. His lifestyle and upbringing were like mine; Black family from poverty trying to "make it out of a beautiful struggle." We were both first generation college students wanting to give our community someone to be proud of. We had many similarities but also differences. Superman's family didn't come from a long history of incarceration and constant trauma of gun violence. Not that it mattered to either of us because our love was strong, but I often wondered how and why he loved someone like me.

My trauma symptoms showed up a lot. From my anxiety and stress of what neighborhood we were in, to what color he wore when we would go out. I remember we were chilling at the house when Superman came in to show me affection and I flinched as a trauma response. He was so mad at me, he expressed over and over how he would never do anything to hurt me. He never ever physically, mentally, or emotionally hurt me. I loved his willingness to talk to my brothers through recorded jail calls, or him not minding that our pictures would be sent to prison. He sacrificed a lot of his time and feelings supporting my need to go to visitations, write letters, phone calls, and be in attendance to court. He never spoke against it. He always showed up with love, as solid as a rock.

No matter how much my relationship had grown with Superman I was always able to show up for my family. I loved the balance it created. I finally felt that I was understood and loved, that I wasn't judged. Like he could come to the family cookout and completely understand why half of the place was empty with only pictures of those who couldn't be there. He always understood, and reassured me that I had him to lean on.

My man, some plans, and my family. I was happy. I started to feel secure. But I knew I wasn't whole. I had yet to discover my "why." My man still cooked for me, and my mommy still washed my clothes. I had only lived in LA and had one perspective of the world. Then, I had a moment. I needed and wanted more.

At the time, I was working at a call center. It was the most fun job I'd had thus far. A lot of young, motivated, supportive, and ambitious groups of people. I met some amazing people there, some whom I still value and love.

During my training I befriended a young, cute Colombian girl. We met and connected instantly. She was fun, loyal, and cool to be around. We bonded and connected over random things but Meek Mill, Nipsey Hussle, and music concerts were the start. She had a way with her words and energy and one evening she persuaded me to purchase Nipsey Hussle's $100 mixtape. Due to my newfound love of the Los Angeles based rapper Nipsey and my loyalty to her I grabbed my credit card, and I did. Nipsey's *Crenshaw* mixtape was purchased, the 62nd of 100 signed copies.

Today, I thank her because that has been one of the best purchases to date for multiple reasons. It allowed me to do something outside the box. Sometimes I found myself sticking to the routine of just work and school. Being more social, going out to concerts and diversifying my friend group was a good thing for me. It also allowed me to play out Nipsey's *Crenshaw* mixtape. I mastered and learned it word for word. It was fun because we would rap the lyrics together. She loved him that much too.

Nipsey Hussle's *Crenshaw* mixtape was my blueprint. I'd liked him before, but this made me admire and fall in love with his vision, his passion, and everything he stood for. The mixtape also encouraged me to revisit all his bodies of work and listen with a different ear. From that point on, I began following his journey as an artist, especially through his videos.

Hey, I can write a whole dissertation on Nipsey Hussle but case in point *Crenshaw* woke me up! It sparked something in me, and made me want to explore my "why." It motivated me to not be ok with just mediocre. It inspired me to leave this world with something I'd never really dreamt of doing before. I never felt I had much purpose; I always knew I wanted to "be something", I just didn't know what.

Nothing had ever really inspired me before besides one of my guy friends who was a graduate of Morehouse College and a traveler. I'll never forget, he took a picture in Japan or Thailand with a lion in his lap and that did it for me. He had inspired me to travel and supported me in obtaining my passport. Yea, outside of that. I hadn't had much. I had no Michael Jordan to look up to or someone at the time I aspired to be like. There were people that I may have come across during my life that planted a seed of hope or motivation, but those connections were only for a moment; no one was ever consistent or stayed.

The thought of that made me sad but it was what it was. When I think about it, I'd only gone to college because it was something I was told I should do. Even me fighting to stay in college, I was told to do. But I was never provided any explanation of the benefits of what college could bring or a blueprint on how to do it. I was just literally figuring it out as I went.

Same with my relationship, I was trying to be the best significant other to my man with no example of a healthy relationship from anyone in my family. I only had sitcom love stories from Mara Brock Akil, and Mary J Blige songs to explain best way to love someone. Again, I was just really trying to figure it out. Finally, finally, I wanted more for myself, other than just being a girl who mastered a love story.

Believe me when I say I quoted Nipsey like scriptures. He would talk about how mapping his plays (goals) were important and how working on them until they came into existence was a success. Through constantly hearing that, I made the conscious decision to really think about what I wanted for myself. I forced myself to sit and from there I wrote my first 'goal's list' at work while I persuaded a customer to enroll in automatic withdrawal (we received bonuses on our check for that).

List:
"Rasheeda what do you want for yourself?"
"Graduate with a 2.5 grade point average.
Lose 10 pounds.
Swim with the dolphins.
Meet Nipsey Hussle.
Get accepted to Clark Atlanta University."

For the first time ever, I thought to myself if you are going to do something, make it great and memorable. I constantly kept hearing about Atlanta, and it had always been a thought of mine to attend a Historical Black College. My second cousin was an alumna of Clark College (before it was re-established as Clark Atlanta University), a member of Delta Sigma Theta Sorority Inc., and someone who's light and energy left a good impression on me. I knew the option of going to Atlanta was a strong possibility. After heavy praying and ongoing discussion with Superman, I had the support behind me.

"Rasheeda bust your butt to obtain good grades. Start taking the school stuff seriously, and then apply to grad school in Atlanta," I told myself.

The decision to apply to and leave the city brought up some intense emotions. What about my brothers? My mommy? My daddy? My nieces and nephews? Damn, my relationship. I had a good man, was I ready and willing to risk the possibility of losing him and the life we had planned together? Who would visit my brothers? Who would make sure our family still had these far and in between family meet ups that kept us in some way connected? Those are the thoughts that I struggled with.

At some point my faith, optimism, and hopefulness was ready to embark on this journey. I had prepared my last undergraduate year in college to make sure I saved every dime. I was proud that I was able to save up $12,000 on my own. I made sure I passed every test and did as much research as I could about Atlanta. I was scared but excited. I'd always dreamt about getting away and I could not back out now.

My last eight months in Los Angeles, I started to dream more. I started to volunteer and give back more of my time through community work. Due to my experience with incarceration I decided to engage in an internship experience working with "at risk youth" as their probation officer. PO Jones is what my supervisor called me. PO Jones absolutely fell in love with the opportunity.

I had a caseload of young boys aged 12–17 who would meet with me at least twice a month to follow up and check in with me as a requirement of their probation. We went over their grades, behaviors, and any community service they had to complete. I always highlighted and acknowledged any progress they had made. Probation officers work with the law but I personalized my experience and made sure I never felt I was against my boys. I remember growing up my twin's probation officer was very calm and laid back. A Black older man who appeared to have my twin's best interest at the time.

He would say, "Do what you are supposed to do, and you will be good." I must be honest; he was one of the reasons I had considered the position.

As I fulfilled my daily tasks as an intern probation officer, I found myself displaying similar calm and laid-back characteristics as my brother's old PO. It wasn't that I did not take my role seriously, it was just that I wanted to be as down to earth, transparent, and calm as I could be. The world was already at these young boys' throats and I didn't want to be another one added to the list. So instead of PO Jones I was Ms. Rasheeda to them.

Ms. Rasheeda the PO you could count on to have a smile, the PO you could count on to remember your favorite rapper, color, subject in school, and hobbies. The PO who looked at the case and situation with the glass as half full rather than empty. The PO who looked at these young boys as soon to be young men of the future. I looked at them with hope and as human beings, not just some case file number assigned to Los Angeles County Probation.

After that experience I held at least two other volunteer positions that allowed me to be a leader for the youth in Los Angeles and provide services to both young boys and girls. I was able to provide these young kids with hope and connect with them by being present, asking them questions, and sharing my story and similar experiences of being a first-generation college student. Working around students especially with similar backgrounds was rewarding. I always left those experiences joyful. During my encounters, I would get random notes and cards from students that I'd worked with. To my surprise they would often share similar sentiments.

"May the Lord reward you well for your kindness you have shown Samuel 24:19. Rasheeda, it was a pleasure to have you as my lead. You're a very kind person. Thank you for taking care of us. You did an amazing job. More than was expected. Thanks for giving us more of your time."

Those notes were appreciated, and made me feel that sense of purpose I'd been talking about. I was doing something worthwhile for someone other than myself or my family. I was giving my time, energy, and a part of myself to a community of youth who would be leading our next generation.

"Be who you needed when you were younger," they say and that was who I was becoming. It was starting to mean more to me than I'd ever been prepared for. This is what I had been longing for, my "why."

Fast forward things were looking up for me. I was excelling academically, contrary to one of my professor's beliefs. I had a White older and very experienced professor at my undergraduate university who held an important position in the social work department and was pretty popular. If she was paying any attention to me, she could have watched me do a complete 360 from the time I took her class up until graduation. I remember I'd failed her class and had to retake it due to some personal matters I was experiencing. As a social work professor, I thought she would be empathetic; a supportive professor, a professor willing to help me problem solve as she witnessed my struggle.

That was the semester when at least two of my friends were killed by gun violence. In addition, I was retraumatized during one of her lectures where she'd instructed us to watch a documentary about Emmett Till and how he never received justice. I still can't believe his killers got off and that the jurors came back with a verdict in less than an hour! The professor never even asked how we felt or explored and processed what that meant to us. It was just another thing to memorize for a test. Do you think I had any capacity to retain or regurgitate any information for her quizzes or tests?

She briefly pulled me to the side and told me "Maybe this class isn't for you. Maybe social work is not for you. You can drop the class now and receive a withdrawal grade and give your spot to someone who is ready."

My heart fell into my lap. What did she know? I wasn't asking for any sympathy or handouts from her; just a little motivation, hope, and a strength's-based approach to pass her class would have sufficed. I was a student, but I was also a human being; a young adult isolated in the back of her classroom mourning the loss of Black bodies. It was apparent she did not know me. I came to terms that that was not okay, but I accepted it for what it was at that moment. I didn't need validation from this White lady, but from that moment on I knew I was going to show her I belonged, and she was going to see it. I ended up passing her course with a C grade.

That was good enough for me; after that day I successfully maintained a 3.0 grade average. I even became the secretary for our social work club on campus. Students trusted me, I made sure my name was on everything and that she would see it. Funny, that my overcompensation in trying to prove this White lady wrong only contributed to me adding and discovering the light that I always had within. I gave her too much power and turned around all things for good.

I left that college with all A's in my last semester and a beacon of hope from my EOP (Educational Opportunity Program) and Pan African Studies program. This first-generation college student was no longer a statistic and guess what, she was on her way to graduate school at the illustrious Clark Atlanta University.

"*Rasheeda Imani Jones, it is with pleasure that we accept you into the Whitney M. Young School of Social Work program.*"

It was official I was going to the "A" aka Atlanta, Georgia!

I was all packed up and ready to go on my vacation to Miami and then my new home in Atlanta. People showed me a huge amount of support and love and I was grateful. My last gift was an experience I would cherish for the rest of my life. I was randomly asked to accompany a good friend of mine to dinner. I couldn't pass up the opportunity. As busy as I was and as much last-minute preparation I had to do, my intuition told me to go and enjoy some last moments in Los Angeles with my friend. I'd be lying if I said I didn't second guess it or complain about how much traffic I had to sit in. The ETA was well over an hour to get to her on a Wednesday night driving towards Hollywood. If you know you know.

An hour later, I arrived at what appeared as a warehouse. I parked and walked into the address she provided. I trusted my friend. If she had said the sky was red. I would do whatever to justify as to why she said the sky was red. I didn't question her. I didn't question why we weren't at a restaurant, where the food was, or why the heck we were in this unfamiliar place. I just smiled and allowed the night to be what the night was gone be. We talked, laughed, we vibed. In walked a familiar face and we continued to vibe. At one point I had to pop a breath mint to kill the hunger and rumbling noises in my stomach. I had given up on going to eat awhile back. As I started to become restless in walks none other than ...

Nipsey Hussle!

"AHHHHHHHHHHH!" (screams excitedly).

The amount of joy that I experienced in that moment was surreal. I could have screamed, cried, jumped but I maintained my composure.

"AHHHHHHHHH!" (screams excitedly).

I'd spent all summer making every effort to meet Nipsey and here I was standing in his studio.

"AHHHHHHHHH!" (screams excitedly).

That moment I'll hold in my heart forever. The more people I met and learned about, the more people I started to admire. How often can you say you met someone you deeply admired. He had inspired so much of my recent growth and so many of the current decisions I had made. He was down to earth and very humble. A real South Central Los Angeles native. So much of him reminded me of my brothers. I met Nipsey y'all.

"AHHHHHHHH!" (screams excitedly)

I am still in awe at how it played out. God will give you the desires of your heart if you ask Him. I was able to share with Nipsey some of my stories, dreams, likes, and plans for travel and career. I even got to show him a video that Superman had documented of me that was inspired and guided by his song "Bigger Than Life." We both laughed at how I decided to skydive in my *Crenshaw* shirt with TMC (The Marathon Continues) written on my hand with a black sharpie marker. His song "Bigger Than Life" brought the emotion to every action that I'd documented. It made you feel me. I ended the night with a picture of us captioned:

"This is dedicated to everybody out there with a motha f*cking dream. F*ck what they say, do your sh*t."

After that night my admiration only grew for him because he was who he said he was. I left my last night in Los Angeles inspired. I felt like Nipsey co-signed all of what I knew Atlanta was going to bring out of me. I felt like I was leaving with the key to the city!

Welcome to Atlanta

Moving to Atlanta was a major move for me. I had never been away from my mom, brothers, or family for more than a month. We were tight like that. The thought of moving to Atlanta was something I'd only dreamt of. Was it really popping like Lauren

London and TI made it seem in the classic Atlanta film *ATL?* Even if it wasn't known for the historical monuments where Dr. King was born, the Black Utopia, and the geographic location of Morehouse, Spelman, and the Illustrious Clark Atlanta University – I think above all the move was necessary for my growth, independence, freedom, and peace of mind.

My life in Atlanta deserves its own chapter, its own book. In the 4 years that I spent there I grew so much. Atlanta is where I became a woman, a selfless woman. A woman of purpose, passion, and poise. In Atlanta, I let my hair down, like let it down. No weave, no nails, no makeup. I embraced every natural part of me and lived life literally to the fullest. I found love in Atlanta; genuine, passionate, fun, and exciting love. I battled depression in Atlanta. Every part of my loyalty, faith, sanity, and existence were tested in Atlanta.

What made me the happiest about my life in Atlanta is that it was all mine. I had no attachments to anyone or anything. I acquired my own friends which was something important for me. Two of my best friends had been friends with my twin brother first. These Atlanta folks befriended me because of whatever they saw in me, and I loved it. From Houston, New York, Florida, South Carolina, and other states I became great friends with people there. I mean I trusted these people with my life, kind of friends. I mean up late at night studying, crying, traveling, and just trying to find a way for ourselves. CAU's motto is "find a way or make one."

My new group of friends had a love for the people, public service, and learned to perceive the world from an Afrocentric perspective. There was no debate amongst us about Black people, Black excellence, Black History, love, education, or the significance of an HBCU (Historical Black College or University). We were all proud to be among a group of the most beautiful people in this world and we would bet our last dollar on it. All the research, hard work, and sacrifices were made with a cheerful spirit. They spoke nothing more than Black excellence and our lives depicted it daily.

Out of my new friends, I found one that I connected with the most. She was my ride or die 'The Atlanta' version. I had the pleasure of sharing all my secrets with her, and she seemed to get every single part of me. Whenever we had to unfortunately justify why Black people deserved any ounce of justice, freedom, or peace, she was right there backing me up. Us together we were unstoppable. We traveled to Ferguson, Missouri to do voter registration together. I liked that she was down to do whatever with purpose and adventure.

Our trip to Ferguson during our 2015 Spring Break was one to remember. We volunteered our whole break, and it didn't even matter that we were housed in a low rated 1-star motel; the fact that we were together made all the difference. We sat in silence for four minutes in honor of Mike Brown in the exact same location where he had laid for four hours after being killed by racist police. We did that together. Rest in Peace Mike Brown, you will never be forgotten.

That same year we scraped up some funds and purchased us a Megabus ticket and headed from Georgia to Washington to DC to be a part of the 20th Anniversary Million Man March hosted by Minister Louis Farrakhan and we did it together. We took road trips to New Orleans and Houston. I remember many nights we sat in the car, library, or our apartment talking and reminiscing about how much of our lives, challenges, and adversity we had overcome. She was my very first friend who turned into my sister. I'll love you forever girl!

I started to cook, clean, and really tap into my independence in Atlanta. I had rarely worked but was fortunate to obtain an internship opportunity that provided me with a $300 stipend to live on for a month which was good for me. I received my food stamps when I did not get a stipend and I found a way to make it work. I was so proud of myself. It was very rare that I called home and asked for anything financially from my mom or Superman. My leap of faith to break away from others brought me joy and pride. Especially Black pride. Atlanta was peaceful. Atlanta was freedom. Atlanta allowed me to never have to look over my shoulder, be conscious of the color men wore, or fear. Atlanta was now my home.

I was quickly reminded that although I was in my new home, my brothers were still back in California in a cell. Innocent and being subjected to more and more systematic oppression. I loved this new woman and became all of whom I aspired to be. Somehow, I lost sight of my brother's freedom, my Superman, and love for my family and community back home. A part of me felt like I had betrayed that part of me. Like in a way I wanted to act like it had never existed. So as much as I loved the new me, I couldn't just write off the old me. I still had the keys to the city, but how could I merge my two lives and make this work?

MOE

You have to face reality to understand that life goes on with or without you. Us behind these walls and between enemy lines are pretty much POW (Prisoners of War). We are inmates on standby usually awaiting or merely hoping for something positive to happen pertaining to California laws. Finding the strength necessary to remain positive or hopeful for that matter, sometimes comes in a roller coaster fashion. Dealing with the different emotions that are formed by the soil of a grave called prison creates a natural imbalance. Due to my current environment, it becomes a task in and of itself.

Spending decade after decade between the confinement of these walls is hell on earth, meant to break every aspect of the mind, body, and soul of a human. Hoping and waiting to receive such blessings (freedom) after so long can easily taint the mind, sometimes making one give up and say "the hell" to the appeal process, positive thinking, and prayers needed to fight this war.

I come from ancestors who are historically rooted in strength, resilience, and who have overcome most things. Although I know and possess that strength it is easy for one to experience false hope, having fought so long and hard for light to shine over our darkened views. Personally, I've always felt that the truth would prevail, eventually setting me free.

As the days on the calendar changed, it became more and more difficult to navigate through the prison walls. However, I knew I could not lose sight and faith knowing I still had a support system who was fighting with me and for me all in the name of truth, even if they were in Atlanta.

Having them with me during this journey has only cemented the spirit needed to fight, live, and win. I mentioned it before, but I really had to process what was going on with those closest to me. My sister had hit a stage where she was blooming physically and mentally, and she wanted to leave the nest and explore and experience life. I can't really recall how it came up or who announced it, but when I heard she planned to leave home to live and attend college in Atlanta it was like a ton of bricks being dropped on me. We'd become so close emotionally that I depended on her in many ways.

Selfishly, I didn't want her to leave. Also, by my little bro and I being incarcerated it would mean that our mom would be alone when she left. I played the devil's advocate with different scenarios hoping a ploy of mine would change her mind. After my attempts I realized the cards weren't in my favor. She left and honestly how could I not want happiness for this young woman who'd been more supportive to me than I'd ever expected? I just knew I'd miss our visits, talks, laughs, and time shared together.

Being that I'm so protective of my queens, the worry and stress would eat me alive if something was to happen to her, but this was an adjustment we all had to make. Now that she was enjoying her new city with her new friends and life, the visits came every so often. Although I missed the visits, I did appreciate that the letters continued, and we had ample opportunity to talk via phone.

I'd ask her a million questions about college, I simply wanted to know. I'm an avid learner so curiosity was eating me up about her subject matters. I wanted to visualize what Atlanta was like. What did she learn? What was college like? What were the students and staff like at an HBCU? She was the only one in our family to attend college so far, so it was the perfect opportunity to expand my imagination. I wanted to know if school was hard and what her future plans were?

Y'all know I asked about her dating. "I'm like what's up with them Country N*ggas? I know you are not attracted to their style?" She'd respond with some sly slick answer just to turn the tide of the conversation.

I'd often ask "Sis, what's up with your friends though?" Sis always had a few cute girls she hung with, but now being in college at a graduate level, I was thirsty for a square. I remember she spoke of her roommate, a girl from the Middle East who was tropical (tropical is another name for a beautiful woman created by our relative Ramone).

My thoughts immediately raced into thinking "Ohhh, I'd kill 'em with her on my side." If I could get my sis's roommate into the visiting room the prison population and correctional officers would be saluting me.

Outside of loving beautiful women, I made it very clear that I love intellectual women. So my sister's roommate, college mate, or whatever friend she hooked me up with would be a triple threat: cute, smart, and foreign. In all my daydreaming, Rasheeda didn't entertain my thirst for her friends the least bit; so much for wishful thinking. She has always been against hooking me up with her friends, which has been our only gripe thus far. Her argument is it'll be a conflict of interest being if her buddy does something disloyal to me, she'll have to address her friend. My sis is a lady and classy but don't get her twisted, she'll flip the switch and go beast mode when need be (don't tell her I told you that).

The college experience was panning out good for her. Mom, our brother, and I missed her and dreaded every time she didn't answer her phone, flew on a plane, or vacationed somewhere etc., all in the name of love. Sis has always been mature, wearing many hats. She can be in Atlanta in school doing her thing but if I text requesting something, she'll multitask and get it done.

She surprised me one time with her generosity. I was being housed in Corcoran SHU (program failure) and during this stay she sent $200 every month and a brief "I love you." She never missed a month. I am not sure how she did it because remember she was a student, so money wasn't plentiful. But she did it and I will forever salute her for it. About a year later, after her monthly offerings she supported me with gathering money from my neighborhood friends to support my lawyer fees.

It was so much going on all the time, that I was overwhelmed with emotion. I was honored that my friends looked out financially, and blessed that I had the opportunity to get another paid appellate lawyer. I don't recall our conversation amid the feelings, but I do recall something like this:

"The homie gave you ___ amount. These homies gave ___ amount. Such and such gave ____. This was the highest amount that I collected," she reported. Then out of nowhere she says "Bro, I've been saving some side money for you I'll match what your homies gave you." I was lost for words. Honestly, I actually had tears forming in my eyes. All I could do is tell my little sis, "I love you Sheeda" and "Thank you."

In prison, unfortunately you become accustomed to disappointment. You numb your feelings, so you won't be vulnerable to anything that'll penetrate your emotions. It's already a constant battle to remain humble, positive, and hopeful in the cesspool so the key to a productive path has been to be both mindful and watchful of those allowed in my space. One thing that this prison did not takeaway is my ability to stay in a state of gratitude. My appellate lawyer was paid and regardless of my negative environment and current reality I refused to let anyone take that away from me. I was reminded that I still had not been forgotten, I was loved.

Alhamdulillah!

CHAPTER 5:
BIGGER THAN LIFE

RASHEEDA

The fact I was able to get out of South Central Los Angeles was by God's grace. He instilled that spark, curiosity, and ambition to want more, do more, see more for myself with no hesitation or regard. I figured if I could muster the courage to go live in another part of the United States for school then I could go abroad and study in another country; and why not in a place cultured, sacred, and close to home – the motherland.

I had no knowledge whatsoever about Africa, South Africa or how to even start the process of going to another country. Fact was I had my passport inspired by a dear friend and a dream. A close colleague of mine from Pennsylvania that I'd met in grad school helped me with this process. It was the way she described her study abroad experience in Korea and Ghana, her shared knowledge, and the fulfilling life moments that she received through studying abroad that inspired and made me that much more eager and willing to go.

South Africa it was! We found a program where the option was to study community engagement and social justice. I didn't quite know what that meant but the word summer, Africa, justice, and a potential scholarship was all I needed to be sold on the opportunity. I did almost everything I could to make sure I would be accepted into this program and spend my summer in Africa! Thank you to everyone who contributed to this experience.

Africa was nothing like I had imagined. Truthfully, I had never imagined. I would see infomercials that would come on late at night. They would display the malnourished children and White people asking for yearly donations (that sometimes helped the children). That's all I'd known it to be. Here and there my dad would highlight the beauty of the continent, or I recall reading about it in some of my Pan African Studies classes, but I could never get those infomercials out of my head for the life of me.

Upon my arrival I was greeted with a host of beautiful students. Looking back, I was so ignorant. Why are all these White people in Africa? I did not come here to see White people. If you know the history of South Africa and apartheid and are knowledgeable about the country, then it makes perfect sense why I was culture shocked.

Anyway, I was greeted by beautiful students with whom I would be spending the next six weeks with. Based on our first interactions and greetings I was pleased and so excited to be exposed to different people, perspectives, and culture. I met a lifelong sister who was a Liberian-American. She was my partner in crime my entire stay. I smile when I think about her. A beautiful brown girl with glasses, full beautiful lips, short hair, and a unique eye for fashion that was so cool to me. Her unique eye for fashion matched her personality. Steller! She was humble, so quiet, so loving, and passionate. A radical for social justice in her own way. Fortunately, not only was she the first person I connected with, but we were also blessed to be paired together when greeted by our host family in the township of Langa. The two of us were on a journey creating timeless memories. They called me Tondakele (Tondakele means the beautiful one in their native language).

As I think of her, I can't help but share the importance of another Black woman I met. She was from Michigan but was a student at Howard University. When I say we connected at the right time and for the right reason I mean just that. My entire stay, she was viewed as my Shero. Shero: a woman admired or idealized for her courage, outstanding achievements, or noble qualities; a heroine. From her natural sponged afro and the way she spoke, to the wisdom she carried; witnessing that love for Black people was very rare to me.

She probably doesn't know it, but she made me feel safe, loved, and seen. She asked me questions no one had ever asked, made me reflect and think of things I'd never thought of, and at one point calmed me down when I was about to lose every ounce of sense I had. She called me her "Mu Chrish." Mu is short for Muslim and Chrish is short for Christian. She came up with this personal nickname for me because I couldn't answer whether I identified as a Christian or a Muslim. I was raised adopting beliefs from both religions depending what side of the family I was with. It was a name I didn't mind being called because I knew her intent, and

I knew where my beliefs resonated. She will be noted amongst the Black women who fought for Black people's liberation like Harriet, Sojourner, Ida, Mary, Dorothy, and Fannie.

I connected with more students who were natives of Ohio, Kansas, New York, Nigeria, and South Africa. They all made a beautiful impact on my experience. They were all well-read, well-traveled, well-spoken, and authentic. Most importantly they had passion for social justice and were interested in change, in a real way.

My roommate, how could I ever forget her? I have had some of the best roommate experiences. From my first college roommate at California State University of Los Angeles to my last at Clark Atlanta, I had known them all to be great women. But this two-day roommate exchange and bonding time were the most meaningful two days I experienced in South Africa.

It had been less than a month since I had lost my dad, so I hadn't really gone through my stages of grief (which you will hear about). There were several nights that I could not sleep, and I cried myself to sleep. There my roommate stood, a stranger willing to be my shoulder of comfort. Not only did we share the physical space of this hotel, but it seemed like God sent her over to me to comfort me and let me know it was okay to release, grieve, and cry over a life and love I'd once known.

She opened that space up but also allowed silence and acknowledged it. I would smile during the day and cry at night, and she never mentioned it after our two-day roommate experience. She did not need to. I had just lost my dad. I didn't have any family or friends at my availability and there she was with love. I thanked God for that experience, to be held during such a vulnerable time, and I thanked her.

Back to Africa. The experience was one to remember. From the food I overate (the fresh skinned meat was to die for, I ate it every day), to the people I met, to every one of the cultural and historical contexts I had the pleasure of learning. I took full advantage.

For the six week stay in South Africa, Langa, Rondebosch, and Woodstock were home for me. This was my family while I learned about social justice and community engagement. Before I tell you about how my experiences in South Africa had a major impact on how I viewed social justice, I must share about my four-day experience as we traveled by van from hostel to hostel through the Western Cape of South Africa.

Bigger than life! An experience of a lifetime! During this four-day adventure I got to step away from my normal routine. I had the option to stay with my Liberian Queen or head to Soweto with my "Mu Chrish" shero from Howard to view Mandela's house, but my spirit led me with a group of six other students to engage in some off-the-wall adventures. We rode elephants and played soccer. The elephants were loving and memorable. We paddled down some river, I dare not know the name. We traveled to take pictures with lions on a safari walk (I still regret not engaging in this activity). We even bungee jumped from the world's highest bridge in South Africa.

Three! Two! One! Bungee.......

I've never felt so free. I jumped from a bridge. We talked about freedom in so many contexts, how sometimes freedom can be defined and sometimes indescribable. Was I scared? Absolutely. However, there were so many shackles and stress I had no control over that were weighing heavy, and I needed to be relieved of them. The adrenalin in that jump gave me a high. I felt free. Free. As I bounced up and down from the elastic that held my feet. I remember crying.

"Daddy, is this what it feels like to be free?"

I noticed the greenery that surrounded me. The air that swept across my face, the blood that rushed to my head. Despite the blood rushing, I took in the moment to swing back and forth in freedom.

Our next adventure was a safari. We were in a jeep. I had always imagined going on a safari and just exploring nature and wildlife and there I was. There were giraffes, zebras, and more lions. Darn it, more lions. During our visit in the Lion's Den our jeep got stuck in a ditch. I swear it was something out of a movie. We were in this jeep trying to come up with alternatives to get us out of this den. I had been praying, but if I had asked God for anything it was to not let me go out to lions!

To make matters worse I had just started a detox earlier that day, so I had to use the restroom almost every half hour. I almost pissed my pants. The lions would look and walk over to our bus then go back to minding their business. My Ohio family offered her water flask as an option for me to use the restroom in, and I took it. It was either publicly show my goods and use the restroom on the back of the safari truck or walk around with wet pants. I chose the latter. I took the risk and used the restroom and within five minutes we were rescued by another jeep. The lions never even came close.

I had the time of my life, and it was fun. Impulsive, scary, yet exciting. I couldn't wait to share my experiences with my brothers. They would clown me and say "there you go doing White people stuff" jokingly, but to me it was an adventure.

I had lived so much of my life feeling trapped that I was willing to try almost anything that allowed me to feel free. It was an experience like I'd see on TV, to share with others. Experiences like these were not accessible where we come from. Surely, there were no wild or fearless adventures in LA. I knew for sure the pictures and my letter detailing this experience would be right on time.

We returned to our home in Rondebosch, Cape Town to get back to learning about social justice and community engagement. As students we were provided a list of options of where we wanted to volunteer as a program requirement. If I recall correctly; homeless shelters, advocacy work within prisons, health, and food distributions were amongst the options we could select from.

Right away I knew I wanted to be a part of whatever community engagement opportunity allowed me to be on the other side of the coin. I was used to being a visitor to a prison; I came in one way and out the same way. While back at home in the states, the overseer/guards/modern day slave patrollers are often what we'd call them. They looked at visitors in a negative light and were rarely nice to us. This time around I got to be a volunteer, work, and get different access and perspective. I was eager to see the difference in my experiences when visiting a prison.

"Who wants to volunteer for Pollsmoor Prison to teach life skills to those incarcerated?" we were asked by our instructor.

"Me!" I was probably the first to raise my hand.

"Ok, well you must go through a process of approval to enter for safety, policy and procedures." Oh, that's easy I thought. I have no warrants, arrest history, or anything. Sure enough, I was approved. We had brief etiquette instruction on how we needed to behave, respond, and act as we were about to start our journey inside Pollsmoor Prison. I'd be lying if I said I wasn't scared, especially when we were told that we would be mixed with a crowd of innocent and guilty inmates, and that we would not know who we were interacting with – we just had to interact.

I had a moment to put things into perspective. How would you want people to view your brother if it was the other way around? Human? Like a person still worthy of love? Someone worthy of a genuine interaction despite any decision that they had made prior to being placed in prison. That was all the time and perspective I needed. I replaced my fear and doubt with optimism and grace, and I was ready. Pollsmoor Prison, I am here!

Six volunteers, our instructor, and approximately 10 men who were incarcerated all gathered in a group. We sat amongst each other engaging in icebreakers that allowed us to get to know each other. My favorite icebreaker was when I was able to put them onto Nipsey Hussle. The moment the men learned I was from Los Angeles they had numerous questions about Kendrick Lamar. King Kendrick was a hot commodity in South Africa, but I knew very little of his music. So, I took every opportunity to tell them all about Nipsey Hussle. From Ferguson to South Africa if you knew me you knew Nipsey. The Hussle Way. I bet you any kind of money that someone today can reflect on me sharing about Nipsey and his influence on today's world.

Our icebreakers were a huge success. In this intimate circle we got to learn about each other, the men's lives, and their challenges. We talked about what made them smile. It was a good feeling to watch them laugh as we completed a team building activity. In this activity specifically we had to trust one another. We had to physically work together, communicate, lean on, touch, and trust one another to successfully complete this activity.

I noticed some of the discomfort in the faces of the students and I noticed a great deal of hesitation with the trust and interaction of the men incarcerated. All bias, discomfort, or fear was conquered. Before you knew it there was a host of laughter and smiles in a dark room full of joy. It was an introduction to our life skills activity, and unfortunately it was our last. Due to unforeseen circumstances, we couldn't return to our volunteer site but the impact it left on us was special. The one day of interaction was enough for all of us involved to be fulfilled.

"I can't wait to tell my brother about this."

I was in a whole prison with people in another country. Real bars, no windows, no air condition. Segregated by klans like the states, based on the tribe and color of your skin. This experience gave me more to talk about with my brother, and also sparked an interest to want to fight racial inequality, injustices, oppression, and those impacted by incarceration a little bit more than before. Each new experience introduced me to something I had an interest in, that I just hadn't fully tapped into.

Being in that prison on the other side showed me how flawed the justice system is around the world; how oppression is oppression no matter where you go, and how every person on this earth deserves second chances, love, mercy, and grace.

I learned that what brought a lot of men to prison in Pollsmoor was not their choices alone. A lot of it was due to trying to survive and meet their basic human needs.

Boy was I ready. I left those men that day with a joyful but heavy heart. When I saw them, I saw hope. I also saw my brothers and my friends back home who were experiencing the exact same systematic oppression and confined to a cell.

It's crazy the way things align. My thesis that I'd been working on for almost nine months was centered around how incarceration had an impact on other people's mental health and their overall well-being. The experience in South Africa was a moment of clarity. I knew I picked the right topic to research, and I had a whole bunch of personal life experience.

Reads text message from daddy:

"*I believe that this or any other global foreign trip for you, can only expand, broaden, enhance your overall view and understanding of yourself and the world in which we live. Love you lil sista! – Yo pops."*

Once I received an understanding of community engagement and social justice from a non-European perspective, it excited me to return to the states ready to stand for something other than myself. Something bigger than life.

Dashikis, Kente cloth, and 15 extra pounds from all the Braai lamb and mielie meal pap is what I'd developed a new appreciation for and took pride in. Six weeks was a long time, long enough that I had found a new appreciation for life and a connection, gratitude, and love for the African Diaspora.

Before I left Cape Town, I made a promise to myself. I was on Robin's Island where I silently prayed near Mandela's cell. "God in this very cell. Mandela sat for over 20-something years. I pray that one day you allow my brother to see his freedom. Justice for Omar."

I shed tears and promised from that day on that I would do some personal and collective work, like Mandela and other political prisoners. I would fight for justice by any means necessary.

Promises are sacred. My promise would be kept.

MOE

As the struggle continued behind these walls, there was a struggle happening on the outside. My homies were getting killed at an alarming rate. My little homies were receiving life sentences at an alarming rate. My little bro and my baby girl, my daughter, were both incarcerated and sadly a few family members passed away. After 16 years I finally got transferred to a prison close to home. Kern Valley State Prison would be my next temporary move. Kern Valley is near Bakersfield, CA which is approximately two and a half hours away from Los Angeles.

This transition was a blessing for us inmates and our families. Having experienced being in a prison where visits were a rare sighting due to the distance and travel fees, being in an institution close to home was a relief for sure. My family could come visit me a lot more and I could now challenge women friends with visiting me. Due to me having been so far from my home city, it was rare to receive visits that the heart desired. Being up North for a long duration of my captivity, these women had righteous excuses and reasons for not traveling so far. But now I'd see who really cared enough about me, because if two hours was too much time to set aside for someone you said you loved, then that wasn't a love I was willing to accept. Naturally I knew I'd have to disconnect with them.

Being down south tends to maximize your opportunities. I'd been fortunate to have had cool runs and bless others due to the blessings of my supporters and family. If we're in contact and you were to reach out for a financial favor, I'll extend my hand; simply because I'm conscious of the everlasting struggle that clouds and smothers those of us imprisoned. I've had cellmates who'd lose their entire families to drugs, the streets, death, or mere nonsupport.

By choice, I only paired with cellmates who I felt would ride for me, no matter what. I only rode with ridas. I always felt that my ridas were people who remained true to the honor and integrity of what we believed in. People who shared similar beliefs. A 'rida' to me was a man who would naturally be aligned on all levels, and most importantly maintain usalama (meaning security & safety in Swahili – a language the Blacks often use in prison to communicate).

As my current reality sat at a standstill, my sister was making moves and taking full advantage of life. My sister was living out her goals and dreams. Pictures would arrive and they'd bring instant gratitude and satisfaction. She went from hitting states to going to theme parks. Transitioning her mind had her ready to travel, so now it was Africa, Cuba, etc.

My body may be shackled up in captivity, but my mind has always remained free. I've lived through my sister's journeys and experiences. She opened my eyes and mind to worldly things that she'd take part in, like skydiving, bungee jumping, shark cage diving, rock climbing, zip lining, horseback riding, just adventurous things I once considered "White people sh*t."

When you're trapped mentally and physically, ghetto bound ignorance has a way of prejudging and denying yourself sheer satisfaction. Well, when these vacations would come up my mom would always pre-speak on it. She would say things like "Sheeda plans on going here or there" so it would naturally spark my interest to want to support her financially without any dilemma. I felt the least I could do was make a financial sacrifice to see to it that my sister could travel and experience another part of God's creation. Of course, I'd like to do more but we both believe that in time Allah Almighty will grant us opportunity to travel together.

It always makes me feel good to be able to support my loved ones. It eradicates the insecurities these prison walls create. As a man we're taught to provide and protect, but being imprisoned, we're paralyzed from doing certain tasks to our standards. Often times we become dispirited with our dignity being ridiculed and slandered by politicians, stereotypes, and just cruel people. Who likes being dependent? I'm certain anyone would agree that sometimes he or she feels awkward asking for things. Now quadruple that awkwardness. That's how many prisoners with self-esteem feel about relying on others.

Prison will strip you of your identity, personality, morals, joy, dreams, and soul if you allow it. So in all actuality, I was killing two birds with one stone by observing my sister's happiness because I was overjoyed as well. My homies in here stayed saluting my sister's life journey and many accomplishments. Sheeda gives the young Black princesses in the ghettos, slums, and project housing an incentive to get up and get out of their current situation. Both my little sister and I would love to be the motivation needed to cure mental diseases that hinder escape – whether that be gangs, prison, drugs, homelessness, abusive relationships, or negativity in general.

"We're all we have," is what my younger homie wrote me as I faced a crisis. His words affected me because I felt his genuineness. These types of homies look out for my sister and respect her desire to become a luminary, which isn't a regular occurrence coming out of our slums. If Sheeda ever asked for a monetary loan, it's awarded because it's going to a positive person. I fully support her efforts in engaging in anything that is bigger than life.

CHAPTER 6:
BLACK AUGUST

RASHEEDA

If there was anything I wanted spiritually, it was to have a deeper connection to my lineage and where I stood as a Black woman. As of today, there is nothing more satisfying than knowing who you are, where you come from, and being proud of that. For so long, I lacked substance and had little interest in what it meant to be Black and a young girl growing into a woman. I didn't understand the power in both.

My dad was a former Black Panther in the Los Angeles chapter and followed the teachings of the Honorable Elijah Muhammad. When I was younger, he adored that I wore a Kente cloth around my neck each morning in the 4th and 5th grades following my teacher's leadership. Growing up there were moments when I would eventually come to hear more and more about America's most influential Black leaders from my father; however, those moments only made me aware, not deeply informed.

My dad would affirm and reassure me that I was a "bad lil sistah" who had a sharp mind, and someone who could accomplish anything as a descendant of Black people.

He would say, "Up all mighty people accomplish what you will!" honoring Marcus Garvey. He would send me random text messages sharing the importance of the Ten-Point Program created by the Black Panther Party, and share his interest in political involvement abroad in the African diaspora. As he talked or texted, I made note that I came from a powerful group of people, but I did not know the depths from which this power came. Does that make sense? I often wondered where my power lied. It never really occurred to me that the power I possessed was rooted in greatness.

My ignorance of the complexities and triumphs of the Black experience made me want to develop a rich understanding of my culture and own it, despite the negative things I'd witnessed growing up. It was important to instill and profess that as a Black woman I had power, but this was a process.

As I matured with new experiences, my relationship with my brother contributed to a deeper level of thinking, which prompted me to want to deepen our relationship. If you noticed, we've been here before (me wanting a deeper level of connection as I age). Time and experience will do this to you. As previously mentioned, whatever he read I wanted to read, whether it was Michelle Alexanders' *The New Jim Crow* or discussing Mansa Musa, Nat Turner, Sojourner Truth, Fannie Lou Hamer, Gaddafi, and countless others.

I made a mental note of the people he mentioned, particularly his request of wanting to grow wiser and better for his personal development. Each time he mentioned anyone I'd never heard of I would take a pen and jot it in my notebook. I had notebooks of scratch paper full of his and our father's honorable mentions. I enjoyed and looked forward to going on Google or YouTube to research people and learn more about them. My big brother was maturing, growing, and sharpening his mind right before my eyes.

Both of my brothers reminded me of our father in the way they thought and spoke, and I enjoyed that part of them. During this phase in our relationship, it appeared as though we both needed what we were giving each other. Which was the ability to plant seeds, seek knowledge, and share ideas. As the saying goes, "iron sharpens iron." I yearned for more knowledge and the ability to connect with him, especially going into my second year in Atlanta. Here it was that reading and critical dialogue would bridge the gap.

Let me take you back for a second to acknowledge someone who planted a few Pan African seeds for me. This will only take a second.

I recall it being the second to last year in my undergraduate program at Cal State LA when I decided to declare Pan African Studies (PAS) as my minor. The objective for the PAS department was to deepen the intellect of students and encourage us to be a resource and change agent in our community for oppressed people. This is where I was exposed to more knowledge, and where seeds were planted.

Dr. CRD Halisi was a scholar, activist, and an educator. I had the pleasure of taking one of his courses as a requirement for graduation. As I sat in his small class of no more than 10 students, I remember how welcoming he made me feel. I had a difficult time at Cal State LA as a minority and first-generation student, but this professor taught me what it meant to be a critical thinker. He would give me several assignments and return it back to me with the same message written. He would give me my full participation points, but my inability to not get deep in my readings always landed me with a B on my assignments.

One day, I stopped by his office hours and was honest with him expressing my concerns of my average grade and his remarks on my papers.

"What do you mean by critical thinking Dr. Halisi?" He took his time to explain to me the objective of critically thinking, the importance, and why we must be critical thinkers in all that we do.

I'd like to say that Dr. Melina Abdullah who was the chair of the Pan African Studies department and one of my professors at the time, made me fall in love with activism and kept me grounded in my work for the community. I followed closely behind her actions in the Black Lives Matter movement when Trayvon Martin's case verdict was read, and worked side by side with her teaching third graders about Kwanzaa. But it was Dr. Halisi planted the seed. It was Dr. Halisi who empowered me to make my mind that much sharper and ask questions that would advance my journey, and develop a great sense of pride for literature, culture, my community, and for myself.

Fast forward, a big brown box arrived with 'P64961 Property of Jones' written big on it. The box sat there for weeks. There was no excitement that the jail had sent my brother's property home. I looked at it as just a reminder that my brother was being sent to the SHU, again! A painful reminder of another traumatic experience of sitting in a small cell counting sheep, lines, and anything else to make the time pass by.

One Saturday, I decided to open it just to feel as connected to him as I could. The scent of his tank tops was calming to me. I enjoyed exploring the type of food that he liked and the different pin up 'Jet Beauty of The Week' photos that were in his property. I smiled big to see the range of beautiful brown women that he was attracted to. I threw away the plates, cups, and things that could not be used and set aside the pictures and letters to resend upon his release from the SHU.

There were tons of books. I was thoroughly impressed. Books dating from the 1997 Million Man March, self-improvement books, and books that provided historical relevance. At that time, I had no desire or capacity to read them. So, I quickly gathered the books and set them on the table for decoration and proceeded with my day. My job was to connect with his belongings and then clear space.

One weekend while I was visiting home from graduate school, I was scheduled to visit a childhood friend of mine who was up North in prison as well. I'd made a commitment to my friendship with him that whenever he was on my heart I would visit if I had the time.

I had started to annoyingly complain to my mom about the clutter in the living room from the books that I'd stacked months ago. They were just there collecting dust. One by one I tossed them, looking for a book to take with me on this two-hour visit to see my childhood friend. I grabbed a book at random, *The Assassination of Fred Hampton: How the FBI and the Chicago Police Murdered a Black Panther* by Jeffrey Haas and dashed out the door.

The drive up the highway was nice. I bonded with my friend's dad talking about the way of the world and how nice it was or how cold it could be. I'm not going to lie, I was honored to keep my commitment to myself by visiting my friend in prison, but to see the joy on his dad's face that his son had a loyal and trustworthy friend felt good. The conversation started to dwindle as there wasn't much left to explore, I opened the book in hopes that the time would pass faster. Opening that book by Jeffery Haas was one of the wisest decisions I'd ever made thus far, here's why.

Fred Hampton was someone whose story made me connect deeply with literature. I'd had my experience of being connected to literature in nonfiction novels, but the Chairman's story had me glued to my seat. Reading his story made me want to learn more about the Panthers including Huey P. Newton and Angela Davis, and know more about revolutionary leaders. It reminded me of COINTELPRO and how destructive they were to the Black community. This book gave me insight to a world that I'd heard of from my dad but was very hesitant to enter (I am still unsure of my hesitancy at the time). As I concluded his book, I felt that I'd wasted so much time of my life in ignorance, even though the opportunities were presented to me so many times.

Fred Hampton was a Black American activist and a revolutionary. He was brave, raw, authentic, prominent, and dedicated his life for social change. He was a young leader in his prime and a radical. He was a loving husband, brother, and son. He was gifted and talented, someone who organized and gave so many of his early years for the people. His life was cut short at the age of 21 when he was murdered by the FBI and Chicago Police as he slept peacefully. I cried reading his story and thinking of what he could have been. But there is also a sense of strength and fearlessness that comes over me whenever I think of him.

"If you dare to struggle you dare to win." – Fred Hampton

Did I mention that Malcolm X was someone that I'd been drawn to? Outside of my father giving my twin brother the name Malcolm as his middle name, it was something about Malcolm that reminded me anything was possible. Spike Lee's film about Malcolm X is in my top three movies of all time. Next to the infamous love story "The Notebook" and "The Lion King." It was something about reading Fred Hampton's book that influenced my desire to read about more Black influential leaders who contributed to the freedom struggle and Black power movement.

They say if you want to hide something from a Black person then put it in a book, and I wanted that saying to cease. So, I ordered The Autobiography of Malcolm X and took it with me to South Africa; my goal was to complete it during my six-week stay and I did. As I read it, I gained a lot of perspective as a student, a young Black girl, and someone who could relate to Malcolm's life.

The love, joy, admiration, motivation, and inspiration I received from reading this autobiography made me want to expand more as a learner. Learning about Malcolm's transition from a life of crime as Detroit Red, to his adult life as Malcolm X, to El-Hajj Malik El-Shabazz was admirable and worth every acknowledgement. His life has shown me that no matter where you come from or what you experience, you have the power to change your life's trajectory with optimism, hope, and faith.

If you don't know, El-Hajj Malik El-Shabazz was a minister, advocate, teacher, husband, father, and friend. He was humorous, full of life and energetic, committed and dedicated to the empowerment of Black people. For me, when I think of Malcolm, I think of most young Black men I see in the streets of Los Angeles. When I think of Malcolm I think of my father and my brothers full of hope, ambition, vision, love, but so much misunderstanding.

As Black people, we are placed in certain circumstances where we have no choice oftentimes but to fight. Fight for power, respect, freedom, liberty, and sometimes for basic necessities. Then America says that we become the product of our environment. What America does not acknowledge is that we possess a lot of wisdom, knowledge, skill, creativity, and that we truly can determine our own destiny if only allowed access, equity, and opportunity.

I truly believe it takes the right person to bring that out of you. Malcolm obtained his master's degree by educating himself in prison. I think of Malcolm often and become emotional. I wonder how advanced and empowered our communities would be if we still had a plethora of selfless leaders like him. Then I snap out of that thought and I look at my brothers. To my brothas, you too can be all that you want to be.

"You can't separate peace from freedom because no one can be at peace unless he has his freedom." – Malcolm X

'Hands off Assata' was a hashtag on social media a couple years back. I didn't join the trend because to be honest I was not familiar with who she was; others knew exactly who she was and her contributions. I had returned to Atlanta after a long summer in Los Angeles. I was two books in of Black Literature, fresh from the motherland, and found myself feeling good about my growth. I was proud to say I had spent a summer in Africa and had the chance to break bread with families who had a deep love for me. I soaked up knowledge, read books, engaged in deep dialogue, and on some nights defended myself and my character as a Black American woman.

There were many nights I debated with one of my "African brothers" about how Black Americans are portrayed in the media and why all Black American women do not behave like Sha-nay-nay (one of the made-up characters in Martin Lawrence's show *Martin*). Some nights those debates made me go to my room anxious, furious, and sad – but I always stood my ground. I was not as confident at the time to have a strong debate, but I knew I was always going to defend Black people.

Fortunately, I came back a better version of myself. My second year in graduate school started and I had tagged a note on my television that read "Turn off the TV and read a book."

Most people were annoyed with me for that (chuckles). I made a conscious decision to invest solely in reading and developing more research for my thesis paper that was required to obtain my master's degree. I looked forward to taking this next level of my academic process seriously so I could finish strong.

One day, while I was in work mode, my new roommate (who was also a Liberian young woman in an undergraduate course at Clark Atlanta) suggested I read *Assata: An Autobiography* by Assata Shakur. Aside from the random talks that my roommate gave me I admired her for her intelligence and hardworking, genuine spirit. I trusted her suggestion of this book and started it immediately. She didn't even know my spirit needed this suggested reading. When she gave me this book I was in a tough spot. Although I had come back to Atlanta renewed with new experiences and more consciously aware and inspired, I was still mourning the loss of my father. Reading Assata took my mind off my heartache for just a while, but it was enough.

Assata Shakur is a beautiful woman; fierce, educated, powerful, brave, dedicated, wise, a woman focused on the liberation of Black people. Assata's book was finished within a month considering my busy schedule, but it was completed at the perfect time. I was writing my thesis on the effects of incarceration and coincidentally was also headed to Cuba for more community engagement with Morehouse College. I feel like as the days went by, I was developing my voice as a woman, finding a place in the fight for social change on a larger scale, and developing a sense of pride that I had longed for. Simply put I was now feeling Black and proud.

Assata, no doubt, is undeniably the truth because of her contribution to civil rights and activism. Traveling to Cuba right after reading her book was full circle. When I was in Cuba, I prayed to run into her, embrace her with love, and tell her thank you. As I was there, I reflected that Omar had shared his tattoo of Assata over 10 years ago during one of our very first visits. He had worn his tattoo of Assata, and I now shared the love for her that he did. I always look forward to being in spaces where I am given the opportunity to chant,

> *"It is our duty to fight for our freedom.*
> *It is our duty to win.*
> *We must love each other and support each other.*
> *We have nothing to lose but our chains."*
> –Assata Shakur

I knew the system was flawed but the exposure of it gave me more reason to be radical in my desire for change. The more involved and informed I became the more stories I'd come across that reminded me how much grief was attached to liberation.

I was watching the *13th* documentary when I had another awakening that I've never been able to really shake away from. More hurt built inside of me; more tears and strong emotions as I witnessed the many injustices rooted in the 13th amendment across my television screen.

I hadn't known what to expect prior to watching this documentary, outside of a friend of mine saying, "OMG Rasheeda, you have to watch *13th* on Netflix, this is right up your alley."

I couldn't help but to think of the many people I knew: family, friends, and just people near and dear to my soul, who've been victims to mass incarceration across the United States. Watching this documentary not only hit home due to the close ties I have with others who have been imprisoned, but also because I knew those were all real events that occur in the "land of the free." These weren't stories created by the phenomenal producer Ava Duvernay; these were stories that our brothers and sisters across the U.S. had endured.

In this film, there was mention of a young brother named Kalief Browder. I want to take time to honor Kalief. Kalief was arrested in 2010 and accused of stealing a backpack (yes, a backpack) and detained on Rikers Island for three years. Being a Los Angeles native, I've heard about Rikers Island being one of the most dangerous jails in the United States and after watching documentaries and doing research, it is in fact.

Kalief spent more than 1,000 days awaiting trial and 700 days in solitary confinement because he wouldn't accept a guilty plea for a crime he hadn't committed. He was not accused of having guns, drugs, causing any harm, or demonstrating any act of violence; he was held for "allegedly stealing a backpack." The thought of it always ignites anger, frustration, and builds upon the resentment I have developed for the American judicial system. After a dreadful three years in Rikers Island, Kalief Browder was released from jail. Following his release, he later died by suicide at the young age of 22. I reflect and think of Kalief and am reminded how I share similar sentiments to the way I felt for Emmett Till, Chairman Fred, Trayvon Martin, and my brother Omar.

Reading more, watching documentaries, and traveling to places provided insight for me. The more knowledge I obtained the more confident I felt in spaces, especially academic spaces. I would be in class or at an event and loved that I could contribute to the discussion. I have never ever felt deeply connected to anything, but this was changing. I will probably keep expressing how I cannot describe the feeling of being more informed. I'd found a passion and desire and wanting to build more ways to be a part of change, especially in the Black community. How could I be a part of important moments in history?

The 20th Anniversary of the Million Man March: Justice or Else was an event that was imperative to attend. This would allow me to be a part of a monumental moment in history. I came across a flier that had my past professor Dr. Melina Abdullah listed as the speaker.

"I know her!" I said excitedly, "That was my professor in undergraduate school. I want to go."

I immediately called my Atlanta ride or die (friend from Houston) asking her if she was interested in attending. As previously mentioned, she'd become my comrade while in graduate school in Atlanta. We were both getting the keys to our apartment at our student lofts, and she walked up to me and introduced herself. Coincidentally, we were enrolled in the same social work program.

From that day on we were always together. We shared the love of travel, community, family, and we also shared similar sentiments for Black culture. This friend saw the transformation firsthand as I turned from this Los Angeles city girl who did not have a strong foundation of cultural awareness, to this young lady who was blossoming into a woman whose sentiments screamed pro-Black in the way I began to walk, talk, think, and sometimes dress.

She proudly accepted to go with me to Washington, D.C., and it did not matter how we would get there. With that energy and willingness to go no matter what, we booked a Megabus from Atlanta to Washington, D.C. on a tight budget, to witness history. I remember being so amazed at the sight of the many Black men, women, and children who were in attendance. It appeared that people came from all over the U.S. to bear witness to this event.

I witnessed historical D9 Greek organizations, Howard, Morehouse, Tuskegee, Clark Atlanta, and so many other Black organizations in the audience. I was impressed by the structure of the Nation of Islam and the way they swayed and secured the crowd. I smiled at every young child I saw who waved a red, black, and green Pan African flag. Red for the blood that was shed uniting all Black ancestry, black for the people, and green for the motherland connecting us to the land of Africa.

My comrade and I fully embraced the experience. It also meant a lot to me that my boyfriend "Superman" and another good friend of mine went along with us in our journey and supported local Black entrepreneurs by purchasing shirts, bean pies, and everything Black.

The event was followed with powerful words by Dr. Abdullah, Minister Louis Farrakhan, and other community activists. I was honored to be in the company of a community of hope and love of thy neighbors. I would bet my last that almost everyone who was in attendance was there to find solutions to the injustices we faced in the Black community. The 20th Anniversary of the Million Man March turned into me engaging in voter registration drives with the NAACP, to then attending a handful of protests in the name of justice. Whether it was boycotting businesses or standing on the frontline for a cause, I somehow started to be somewhere in the crowd when duty called.

Attending events started to become a thing. I looked forward to going to them, but they had to be intentional, meaningful, and ones that would make an impact. Although some of the events like protests were typically started due to someone losing their life, it always felt good that so many people, especially young people were willing to sacrifice and stand up in solidarity for others. I would look around and herds of people would be laughing, smiling, crying, angry, chanting, hugging or embracing one another. We were all there because we demanded better.

In this journey of deepening my knowledge, I have come to learn about Black August. I'd been having a discussion with Omar and he shared that he would be fasting for Ramadan.

We were talking and he said, "Sis, I'll be fasting for three months. Ramadan, July, and Black August."

He went on to explain the significance of each month and what it all consisted of. I was excited to learn more about Black August as I'd already had my share of fasting for Ramadan in solidarity with my father. My brother provided me a foundation of what Black August was but the scholar in me decided to further my understanding. Black August is a month that honors Black freedom fighters and political prisoners in honor of George Jackson.

"Ok, so who is George Jackson?" I proceeded to type into Google.

"George Jackson was an author, activist, and revolutionary," I kept digging. One Google search turned into the "Soledad Brothers" and another search turned into more information. I found more and more information about the significance of this month and was elated. Black August highlighted Black resistance and racial oppression, and it started in prison with political prisoners. I then came across how other historical events occurred in August. Like the Haitian Revolution in August of 1791, Nat Turner's Rebellion in August of 1831, The March on Washington in August of 1963, and The Watts Riots in August of 1965. These were big events that were significant in history.

August also has the honor of celebrating the births of important Black leaders like Marcus Garvey, Fred Hampton, Dr. Mutula Shakur, and James Baldwin. I was impressed, amazed, and ready.

"Bro, sign me up. Let's do it!"

I was determined to embark on whatever Black August entailed because I knew it was beneficial for the both of us. Our plan was to first understand our why. Why are we doing this? We were doing it for solidarity, discipline, self-love, self-awareness, and love. Then, we decided we would read and workout daily. We had to pick cultural literature that enhanced our knowledge of either America or Africa. I enjoyed how my brother and I would joke about who could lose the most weight within our workouts. I was always up for the challenge. Essentially, Black August allowed my brother and I to deepen our bond while being in solidarity with the Black community and those who are politically aware.

I've come to learn you can sit on social media and write cool posts about the injustice the Black man and Black woman face today, or you can be a part of the change you wish to see. I hope with all respect, sincerity, and truth that this chapter has created an awakening in you, as Black August has done for and to me. I am just getting started.

"I feel safe even in the midst of my enemies: for the truth is powerful and will prevail."
-Sojourner Truth

MOE

We as Africans (Blacks) incarcerated are big on discipline, as it's a major survival tool and method one should implement daily in their lives. Conditioning your mind and body is a weapon, and in prison you never want to get relaxed.

"You stay ready, so you don't have to get ready," is a motto we utilize amidst street trials and tribulations. Well, it's the same sh*t different toilet.

Discipline didn't come too easy for me. I started practicing disciplining once I arrived in prison. In prison we feel like the general population is equal to the streets and the SHU (the hole) is like being in jail. When I started going to the hole it became apparent for the prison program to tighten up. We have a morning and a night roll call. Only active individuals get acknowledged. It's a no talking grace period (speaking isn't allowed out your cell or down the way to neighboring cells). All this is done out of respect, being that we're all men of different races but common views.

We get up at 6:00 a.m., roll up our mats, put our shoes on, take care of our morning hygiene duties and prepare for the day ahead. One may read, write, draw, study, or exercise. It's funny, when I first came to the yard at 23 years old, I wasn't disciplined at all. Waking up early was a constant struggle. So was my conditioning, I wasn't on point physically, so the start of my discipline came with resistance. I'd often work out with the homies who conditioned their mind, body, and soul daily.

We'll have a homie verbally call a routine, in which he'll keep the count in Swahili. Burpees are a common exercise done here, adopted from Navy SEALs or Army regimen. During our workout, there's no talking, spitting, or drinking water during the routine. If one gets winded you must run on the track. If the instructor messes up the count, we all start over. I used to have a fit over the rules due to my lack of discipline over my mind, body, and soul. Once you are invested and committed to discipline it becomes a lifestyle.

I started challenging myself for positive results to show. I stopped eating meat, saying 'blood', gang writing, smoking, and drinking, which were habits I had grown to love. School has always been important to me but with this new desire to remodel and reshape my temple, it was time to tackle another task.

While doing a SHU in Pelican Bay State Prison I requested to take my GED. Let me acknowledge the fact that math was my nemesis; you need a 500 score to pass. It took me three General Education Development pre-tests to finally pass. I remember wanting to give up plenty of times, but discipline played a part in my relentlessness. It felt good to receive my GED years later at Salinas Valley State Prison in waist chains.

Religiously, I'm ardent and eager to learn; being spiritually in tune has always gotten me by. My grams had me in her church well enough for me to claim God as my savior and me as a Christian, but I didn't know much about the Bible. My father practiced Islam and was stern about me following the tradition. My mom must have figured it was a wise choice because we didn't eat any pork, ate healthy, and sat on pillows at a lower table. I attended a private school by the name of Marcus Garvey, prayed at a mosque, and wore Muslim attire. Boy I couldn't stand these rituals, especially when it became obvious my dad was behind this structured lifestyle.

I always thought to myself, "How are you trying to enforce something, but not here to see it through?"

I would complain to my moms about these practices. Mind you, whenever I was at my aunty or gram's house it was the opposite: "freedom is ringing." Big pork chops and ham sandwiches, regular clothes, being able to watch television all night, chilling. The typical child boy activities. Also due to my strained relationship with my father, I clearly grew to rebel against anything he stood for – and he'd been a devout Muslim.

As I aged and began to open my mind in a broader sense, I took to studying the Bible and Quran, attended services, and had literature and *The Final Call* sent to me. When Ramadan was introduced to me its purpose became defined. It went hand and hand with my direct preference. Years ago, I started practicing Ramadan. It felt good to be a part of a positive movement. June, July, and August were now three more months I'd give my mind, body, and soul to.

We also celebrated Black August for the political brothers who've made sacrifices to make living conditions better here in prison – like General George Jackson, Johnathan Jackson, Huey P. Newton, Bunchy Carter, Bobby Seale, Lumumba Shakur, and a sea of other defiant New Africans who shed blood or lost their lives standing up for oppression. When you study, learn, and witness the strength of your people's past and present, it pumps the blood, boils the blood, and lights the human spirit to fight, even if it be "fire with fire." There's no way to accept oppression; accepting it means "no will, no morals, no strength, no fight, no backbone, no manhood."

I've never given into drugs, alcohol, medications, depression, suicide, homicide, homosexuality, or becoming content with dying in prison. The way I've always carried myself here or on the streets has given me a sense of pride, character, and conduct that goes a long way in life, and it's priceless.

The youngsters are paying attention and in the underworld (streets) you don't have many chances to give off bad impressions. In the gang world it's a constant challenge and competition. One day you can be the man, the next week your name is in question over committing an action that isn't respected. So, I push, press, and frontline like I'm under a constant microscope.

I've come too far, dedicated too much while still sacrificing, to allow my deeds to go unnoticed or be done in vain. My name and reputation have been misrepresented. People speak about a lot of wrongdoings and shortcomings rather than go beneath the surface.

On many occasions I've had my homies, mom, grams, aunty, girls, call the prison counselor to state their concerns for my safety. They hear stories of me and believe I'll jeopardize the homie's life or my freedom with reckless ways. If only the prison counselors understood that I'm the one who encourages other incarcerated folks to study and become more than what these prison walls think of us. It's a chapter in our lives we'll all grow out of if we apply our minds. I'd never want anybody to endure these inhumane conditions (wouldn't wish this on my worst enemy). They enclose two men in a six by nine cell, yet it's unconstitutional in California to put two animals in a six by nine cage. We must open our eyes to see the real enemy and problem.

Living amongst 1000 inmates in the compound requires a high tolerance to live and function around so many attitudes, personalities, and egos (both correctional officers and inmates). For me it's natural instinct to study people's behavior and familiarize myself with the yard, as every yard runs differently depending on the strength and weakness of the inmates politicking. It's my duty to have an eye for danger, keep my ears to the ground, and stay security conscious. These rituals are a thug's nature being these are street regulations. I'm on my young homies about security, the TV, radio, and then visits come second. Top priority is our livelihood, so I am a firm believer in practicing discipline daily.

I remember losing my relative Derek while I was housed in Pelican Bay SHU. I had a few months left to do in the hole, after having been back in that dungeon already for 17 months. Originally, they booked me for a knife which carries seven, 10, or 17 months in the hole. Due to it being my second time being caught with a knife (which was for my protection), they gave me 16 months.

After my time was ending the committee deemed me a program failure because I had five months of prior SHU offenses within a three-year occurrence. I gave them another year in the SHU, which had me at 26 months for a knife I had not used. Remember the loss of my relative occurred so I was eager to get back to the mainline to trip. I went to the committee again, only to be told I'd remain in the SHU for an ongoing investigation. Take a minute. Count the months I had spent in the SHU. That does something to you mentally.

The prison staff withheld my mail, took my phone book, and all my property. Oh, how I yearned for someone to vent to. Other prisoners had their own issues to deal with; it's only so much you can expect in return. You couldn't have contact visits or phone calls to your desire, so my options were few.

I went against a rule I abided by for years, which was not talking with a psychiatrist. I signed up for a session and to my surprise it was a healthy experience. She was a White, older, free-spirited woman. She asked about my pain, struggles, goals, and upbringing – typical questions I assumed a psych asked. Around this time my daughter and I were going through her transitioning from daddy's girl into a young lady, and it came with arguments, debates, and resistance. So, it was a lot of baggage I let out on this woman. I recall one afternoon venting to the psych and out of nowhere I heard her whimpering softly. She was crying.

"Aww Lawd," I remember thinking.

She said, "Mr. Jones, excuse me, it's very unprofessional to cry in front of a client," she was supposed to be the strength, director, and guidance amidst my agony and pain.

She said she'd never heard such tragic and painful stories and just became emotional. I told her it was cool and reminded her that she was human, and a job could not control her natural human instinct and interaction. She gave me good advice, we prayed together. She wanted me to read different books, do yoga, deep breathing exercises, etc. This lady helped break the walls I surrounded myself with, when I had stereotyped and prejudged the ability and truth of a psych.

My experience with her changed my opinion about psychiatrists. That lady gave me strength, insight, and human interaction; while these four walls, correctional officers, and the SHU ate away at my soul and spirit daily. I've always thought and reacted as a leader in my world. It's too many sheep in wolf clothing that are used to being codependent, doing what they think is cool, gangster, or will be accepted by hierarchy.

I'll go against the grain if I feel or sense anyone is on some soft or foul sh*t. I am of age now, where respect is my triumph and you can be a Crip, Mexican, White boy, Asian, or Bay Area brother it doesn't matter. As long as you respect the convict g code, we'll have a common underlying status quo. Okay, back to Black August.

The "Sacrificers"

We'll give a lady I admire the spotlight first, Ms. Assata. The mother hen of our revolution. Once I read about her mission, sacrifice, and commitment to the comrades and the people she stole my heart. This Black Queen held court in the streets with the New Jersey pigs and got apprehended. She went down stitched lips even though she was found guilty. While incarcerated her worth was so important that her comrades broke her out, she has been in Cuba for decades listed as one of the FBI's Ten Most Wanted. She loves us Black folks so much and you can tell when you read her publications in prison news lettering.

I remember my people had come to visit me years back and we were at the table chilling when the girls (my sis and daughter) were checking out my tattoos with their nosey ass. Mind you, I have tons of tattoos, but this tattoo was special. I had my neighborhood and fallen soldiers' names tattooed on me, that it was only right that I would get my legs tattooed with something positive. I felt I would combat the gang sh*t they frowned upon. I pulled my pants leg up and showed a big portrait of a lady with an Afro, thick lips, hoop earrings with Africa inside.

My daughter's outspoken ass sarcastically asked, "Who is that your mom?"

I shook my head, proudly announcing "Naw it's Assata."

Of course, I had to educate the table, aside from grams who smiled, approving the act. Around this time, I'd committed to the non-fiction books, primarily history about Africans, Black Panthers, and Black Militias. It was amazing and quite interesting to learn about the many countries within Africa. Our people and languages, like the Bantu, Bangala, Jaba, and Bushongo people, were some active tribes. Black Pharaohs and Nubian Kings ruled over Egypt.

Here are a few notables who stood out to me and caught my interest: King Timbuktu, King Taharqa, King Mentohotep II, and

Rameses II. They ruled dynasties. We have Queens who ruled with an iron fist and engaged the Assyrians and Kush in war. They literally were in an open field with bloody uniforms and fake beards.

Here are a few Queens that stood out whom I salute with much respect: Queen Candace, Toya, Kawit, Hatshepsut, and Fatima. I learned of Sonni Ali, Hannibal the Great, African slaves, Negro bishops, the ivory, iron, gold, tiger skins, trade etc. It's good to mix up your research. We have a long line of history to be conscious of. We're descendants of a beautiful continent you'll love and honor once you research it – Africa.

As a target and victim of the 'New Jim Crow' mass incarceration, it was my aim and duty to execute my God-given "mental powers" which can't be chained by shackles. So daily, I am eager to learn and seek information from both the living and the dead. Shout out Tavis Smiley and Cornel West.

Another brother who was prominent in his time was Fred Hampton. The Chicago Chapter BPP (Black Panther Party) was active, and Fred was front lining the movement by voicing the injustice, racism, and disparity of the people; in the 60s it was way more vital to be a guerilla. Fred opened his home to comrades due to continuous harassment by racist police at the Panther's quarters. Fred's frontline sacrifices, his voice, and opening his home to the people cost him his life. The pigs raided early morning, kicked in the door with guns blazing and shot and killed Fred while he laid with his girl, pregnant and all. The cold part was he got shot over 20 times with no gun found in his possession! Fred never saw it coming.

"Black lives never mattered and don't be duped to think we matter today."

If you readers get the time or opportunity, check out *The COINTELPRO Papers: Documents from the FBI's Secret Wars Against Dissent in the United States*. It's a book exposing the FBI and J. Edgar Hoover and how they targeted the Panthers, doing whatever necessary to disfigure the movement. The law is utilized illegally by lawmakers when it's used against non-Whites. G Man (J E Hoover) had targets on King, Malcolm X, and the Panthers. The book displayed actual Panther leaflets where it was Newton and Bobby Seal feuding East Coast and West Coast beef, but truthfully it was propaganda written by the Feds to divide and conquer. The book is informative, and I recommend it.

You'll see that history repeats itself; the police utilize the same tactics to hunt and take down the modern-day Panthers, Bloods and Crips like they used in the 1960s. Us as Black folks are stubborn and selfish. We're too quick to judge each other, tear down, and literally turn our backs on each other. Everybody has a story of struggle, being that we were conquered amidst a struggle; stolen, raped, overworked, overtaxed, underpaid, and undervalued; but also underestimated, because we still rise. We are all entitled to have our beliefs and philosophies, but in the end, we have to put aside our differences as a race and rise against the unjust.

Behind the walls we are all in our cliques and subsets. Different gangs, constitutions, and politics bring the necessary division among different gangs and cultures; but trust, once a non-Black causes a safety risk it's considered a code red. We mount up like Zulu warriors; it's an alarming sight for anybody.

I'm not promoting violence; I am suggesting that unity and diplomacy should always be our first method. The Panthers have always been a teaching vehicle for me to learn from.

They funded food programs, after-school programs, clothes, school supplies, and educated us socially and politically while promoting self-defense. We policed the police as they harassed our communities.

In my youth as I functioned with the Bloods heavy, I recall the structure and discipline. It was common to have meetings and hold soldiers accountable on many levels for different infractions. It kept a fear factor in play. We'd also go to Jim Brown's house or Minister Farrakhan's public speeches, which would bring forth unity amongst Bloods and Crips and speak on transparent injustices. So, I entered this belly of the beast with the common knowledge and practice of unity, discipline, and structure.

Let's be real with ourselves and each other. It's quite difficult to hold conversations or break bread with an enemy; we were just head hunting each other on the streets. The guerilla warfare I've engaged in literally damaged me psychologically, to the point I remember telling my cellmate who was a double OG who'd been down for 28 years, "Blood I hate Crips more than anybody else," meaning Mexicans, Whites, others, even police.

That's how much gang violence affected my thought process. It was tunnel vision at its finest. Unlike the Panthers and our elders, we've lost sight of our common cause; our self-hate leads us to Black destruction, "The Hate you Give." It took self-healing, self-awareness, self-control, self-seeking, and self-examination to start searching for self-reform. I see in Crips the same hurt, bitterness, hate, negative thinking that I once identified with. It truly takes mental growth to adhere to change.

My father always pressed Black reform. He was intellectual with a particular passion for race relations, Islam, and politics, so the fruit fell into my lap. For the most part my father and I had a distant, distraught, and disingenuous relationship which you will later hear about. I disobliged anything he considered out of spite, hurt, anger, and the mixed emotions of a son who needed a father. Finally in my 30s with spiritual growth and my sister always on my ass, I found forgiveness necessary, and my father and I formed a long-awaited relationship.

My father had been incarcerated regularly so our dialogues started via correspondence from prison to prison. It was an enhancement to receive enlightening literature. My pops was a politicker so his vocabulary spoke of our people's injustice and the solutions one must undertake to see change. Pops was a scholar, warrior, servant to Allah, and a teacher to his children. He didn't agree with my gang lifestyle, and I didn't agree with him being absent, but in the end all his tough love was received in high praise. I see a lot of him in us all (my brother, sister, and I).

We have the keys to our destiny. You get that through education, discipline, and a love for the struggle. I've learned not to ask God the "why" of things but to accept that God is in control of all things. I've embraced my struggles but won't let it define me or control my destiny. The struggle has been going on for centuries; it stems from apartheid, drugs, poverty, gangs, crime, and lack of opportunities.

Us lower-class Blacks in urban areas have experienced the misfortunes of living in slum-like conditions. It's an everlasting struggle for many, but some are blessed to make it out of the ghetto. My salutations for those who have. Those like me have found strength, solace, and appreciation for life regardless of my 26 years of incarceration for a crime I didn't do; regardless of the loss of family, friends, and freedom.

It takes a disciplined mind to accept the current facts. I'm blessed to have family and homies who write, visit, and support me morally and financially, as it takes the heat off me occasionally. For me writing, reading, and exercising are my daily therapeutic rituals. When I was caged in the SHU there was limited interaction and socializing, so I started to write short essays. Let me tell you about a few of them.

The few titles I recall are "Incarcerated Scar Faces", which spoke on past and current warriors locked up nationwide who wear scars and tattoos on their face and body pridefully; a badge of honor for putting that work in. The African tribe used to have scar-like tatts as well to symbolize their valor warfare. The next was called "Rebels Without a Cause", about the generation who are doing this as a fad, influenced by hip-hop, following the Kardashian-type n*ggas.

The young home girl once said to me, "Mad these n*ggas is banging for the draws, not the cause!"

The next short essay I wrote was titled, "My First Love" which was a tribute to the hood. I would say a lot of people's first love is their girl but after being gunned down at 13 and witnessing the pain, anger, love, and revenge for me displayed by the troops, they became the receivers of my first love. The gang world gets a lot of bad press from those who are illiterate or ignorant to our upbringing, our plight, and our movement.

The homies have been influential in me being a father, going to a school, and evolving as a man. The homegirls have always spoiled me with love, affection, and unlimited support. South Central LA is the Mecca of gang culture. You can't avoid having an opinion or being affected, whether good or bad. We're forever receiving negative exposure, the media refuses to highlight the many positive contributions the conscious members do for our communities; food giveaways, toy giveaways, donations, funding little league programs, etc. We give moral support to the non-affiliates who seek to attend college. We always come together with a ceasefire or gang truce when the blood of kids, elders, and innocent people is spilled. Also, we are on the front line when the police abuse their power by shooting, killing, or beating one of ours unjustly.

In my eyes the gangs, primarily the Bloods and Crips, are gatekeepers and vanguards for the people. I'm not a supporter of Black-on-Black crime even though I am aware that violence is necessary and even imminent in certain situations. But in the mix of politics, debates, and opinions the fact is Minister Farrakhan asked for a million brothers to march and trust me, it was the gang members who were on the frontline and made sure security wasn't breached. I'm not downplaying the Muslims or brothers in general who participated, but we're soldiers who keep our uniforms on and just because the naysayers don't relate to our pride for the red and blue flags just remember, we're still Black and proud.

"Power to the People."

The same brothers that you despise, abandon, talk down on, frown upon, will be the same brothers who'll protect you in a dark alley, behind these walls, or in any given situation. So as a reformed man and Blood, I'd like to be given the benefit of the doubt and be judged by my actions instead of my look, being incarcerated, my past, or my street name. You expect the system, non-Blacks, and racist people to have misconceptions of us, but it kills me when your own people speak down, tear down, or give up on you!

Let me get back to studying.

- -

TAWFIQ, ABDUL LATIF Unit: LOS-E-S
DATE: 03/19/2012

DEAREST SON:

MY RESPECTED BROTHER............PEACE AND PROSPERITY THRU STRUGGLE; (STRUGGLE OF THE MIND AND SOUL; AGAINST OPPRESSION & TYRANNY; DECEPTIVE, MISLEADING, AND INFERIOR IDEOLOGIES/BELIEFS; AND STRUGGLE FOR THE SPIRIT TO REMAIN ELEVATED AND HUMANE). LIL BRO', THE JINN/MEN HAVE THROWN YET ANOTHER TEMPORARY OBSTACLE & ROADBLOCK FOR POPS TO OVERCOME. BUT LITTLE DO THEY REALIZE THAT HISTORY AND OUR FUTURE HAS BEEN INTRINSICALLY MOLDED AND FORGED TO WITHSTAND THEIR PUNK ASS BLOWS. FEEBLE INDEED! NOTHING THEY DO SHOULD EVER SUPRISE OR INTIMIDATE US. P.O.W.'S HAVE WITHSTOOD ALL MANNER OF PHYSIOLOGICAL AND PSYCHOLOGICAL TORTURE. SO WE ENDURE AND PUSH/ MASH FORWARD.

I'LL BE 'ON DECK' WITH SISTA RASHEEDA IN EARLY APRIL, ALLAH WILLING, AND WE WILL BE RELENTLESSLY PURSUING THE ATTORNEYS, AS I'LL HAVE MUCH MORE LATITUDE TO MOVE ABOUT W/O ANY MAJOR RESTRICTIONS, YA FEEL ME?? I HAVE BEEN PERUSING CASES RELATIVE TO YOUR OWN OR REMOTELY CONNECTED. ENCLOSED IS AN INSIGHTFUL ARTICLE RE: EYEWITNESS IDENTIFICATION AND ALL IT'S FLAWED PREMISES. SO, WHEN WILL YOU BE RAISING FROM THE DUNGEONS & REAPPEAR BACK IN A LESS RESTRICTIVE HOLE?? BOONIE WROTE TO ME, SO IM GONNA GET BACK

@ HIM SOON. I'LL TRY TO BREAK SOME CHEDDA CHEESE W/U ONCE I'M LIBERATED.

I'M OUT YOUNG WARRIOR, LION/CUB. DID U GET THE BOOK I SENT OVER A MONTH AGO (FRED HAMPTON)??? LET ME KNOW CAUSE THE STATE SUPREME COURT HAS LIFTED, AT LEAST IN PRINCIPLE, MOST FORMS OF CENSORSHIP AS IT RELATES TO SOCIO-POLITIKAL MATERIAL. STAY IN TOUCH. A COUPLE OF THE HOMIES SEND STONE LOVE.

ONE LOVE.........YOUR POPS, ABDUL- LATIF

- -

TRULINCS 76596012 - TAWFIQ, ABDUL LATIF - Unit: LOS-E-S

FROM: 76596012
TO: Jones, Desmond J
SUBJECT: MEE MIZOE....................
DATE: 03/19/2012 12:49:21 PM

MARCH 20, 2012
ABDUL-LATIF TAWIQ
7560 VANTAGE AVE.
NO. HOLLYWOOD, CA. 91605

OMAR JONES #P-64961
SALINAS VALLEY STATE PRISON
P.O. BOX 1050 C-2 #120
SOLEDAD, CA. 93960

DEAREST SON:

MY RESPECTED BROTHER..........PEACE AND PROSPERITY THRU STRUGGLE; (STRUGGLE OF THEL MIND AND SOUL;AGAINST OPPRESSION & TYRANNY; DECEPTIVE, MISLEADING, AND INFERIOR IDEOLOGIES/BELIEFS; AND STRUGGLE FOR THE SPIRIT TO REMAIN ELEVATED AND HUMANE). LIL BRO', THE JINN/MEN HAVE THROWN YET ANOTHER TEMPORARY OBSTACLE & ROADBLOCK FOR POPS TO OVERCOME. BUT LITTLE DO THEY REALIZE THAT HISTORY AND OUR FUTURE HAS BEEN INTRINSICALLY MOLDED AND FORGED TO WITHSTAND THEIR PUNK ASS BLOWS. FEEBLE INDEED! NOTHING THEY DO SHOULD EVER SUPRISE OR INTIMIDATE US. P.O.W.'S HAVE WITHSTOOD ALL MANNER OF PHYSIOLOGICAL AND PSYCHOLOGICAL TORTURE. SO WE ENDURE AND PUSH/MASH FORWARD.

I'LL BE 'ON DECK' WITH SISTA RASHEEDA IN EARLY APRIL, ALLAH WILLING, AND WE WILL BE RELENTLESSLY PURSUING THE ATTORNEYS, AS I'LL HAVE MUCH MORE LATITUDE TO MOVE ABOUT W/O ANY MAJOR RESTRICTIONS, YA FEEL ME?? I HAVE BEEN PERUSING CASES RELATIVE TO YOUR OWN OR REMOTELY CONNECTED. ENCLOSED IS AN INSIGHTFUL ARTICLE RE: EYEWITNESS IDENTIFICATION AND ALL IT'S FLAWED PREMISES. SO, WHEN WILL YOU BE RAISING FROM THE DUNGEONS & REAPPEAR BACK IN A LESS RESTRICTIVE HOLE?? BOONIE WROTE TO ME, SO IM GONNA GET BACK @ HIM SOON. I'LL TRY TO BREAK $OME CHEDDA CHEE$E W/U ONCE I'M LIBERATED.

I'M OUT YOUNG WARRIOR, LION/CUB. DID U GET THEL BOOK I SENT OVER A MONTH AGO (FRED HAMPTON)??? LET ME KNOW CAUSE THE STATE SUPREME COURT HAS LIFTED, AT LEAST IN PRINCIPLE, MOST FORMS OF CENSORSHIP AS IT RELATES TO SOCIO-POLITIKAL MATERIAL. STAY IN TOUCH. A COUPLE OF THE HOMIES SEND STONE LOVE. ONE LOVE......................YOUR POPS, ABDUL -LATIF

CHAPTER 7:
OUR FATHER'S EYES

RASHEEDA

"Hi Rasheeda. Hope your day was a good one. Happy 4 u overall. You're evolving into quite a young woman: one to be proud of. Keep up the positive work. Get @ dad when u r able sis. I'm just trying to heal and stay alive w/ much prayer, hope. I'm blessed to have such a powerful supportive family...love you dear."

–May 7, 2015

I didn't answer the last text message he sent. I wanted to surprise him. I wanted to give my daddy the biggest hug I had in me because it had been at least five months since I last smelled his fragrance and complained about how his salt and pepper beard itched my face. They say daddies are a girl's best friend but for me it has always been my brothers. There was no part of my life I did not have them near, even if it was through a wall phone on a recorded line.

However, from 2011 to 2015 I'd developed an amazing relationship with my daddy. I have so many memories with him when he wasn't in and out of federal prisons. I remember him coming to pick me up from school singing "Oh, Oh Sheeda", remixing the words to "Oh Sheila", the 1985 single by Ready for the World. I would always drag my words, "daddy stop," feeling embarrassed but also loved and important since thinking I had a song with my name in. Nonetheless, the extent my daddy would go through to ensure I felt love was always acknowledged when it mattered most. From my school graduations to my senior prom, and important times that girls reflect on, he was always there by my side. I guess the universe made fit for him to be released from prison when I needed him.

A man of principle, integrity, and commitment. Discipline, wisdom, activism, love, and a very militant presence. He demonstrated good militance, but he also did not play. I remember all we wanted was pork bacon and he refused to go against his beliefs for our desires. His love for us and only wanting the best for us made him that way. He knew that something as minor as pork was a huge no for his kids, it wasn't happening.

A man of morals. A husband, father, comrade, educator, lover of life and all things. He was truly someone I am so honored to be an extension of, despite any flaws or wrong doings that landed so much of his adult life in and out of prison.

"Daddy, get up! I'm here. I had to come by to see you before I got on to Africa. Daddy, get up. I have an event that's coming up with Ava DuVernay at Cal State LA that I know you would love. We can go as my gift to you for your birthday."

I was excited. I had just raised the money I needed to go on my first out of the country experience (the one I just shared), my friend was graduating with her master's degree from USC, and I'd just turned 25 years old two weeks prior. I looked good and felt good and I just wanted to celebrate with my daddy by doing something I knew we would both enjoy.

Surprisingly, my daddy didn't answer back. I climbed in bed with him and laid on his back while he avoided facing me.

"Daddy, what's wrong?" I damn near died on the outside asking him that question.

Internally, I was dying. My spirit didn't sit well especially when I noticed that he was not as excited to see me and avoided looking my way. All those messages he texted me and I failed to acknowledge he was sick! Looking back, my optimism got the best of me. My faith in God would not allow me to think for a second that something was wrong with my dad.

As I laid there with him, he declined my offer to see Ava Duvernay and asked me to get him some sweets to ease his pain. My heart fell in my lap as I walked down to talk to his wife about his health. I was in denial at the thought that he could be sick. I listened to her but was still so very full of optimism, not thinking that our time together was about to end. I thanked his wife and remembered shedding only a few tears, I hopped in my car thinking and knowing "my daddy is going to be straight."

Two days later, I received a voicemail from my older sister that I had to come say goodbye to my daddy, as he was dying.

I remember like it was yesterday. Saturday, I was sitting in Benihana's Restaurant celebrating my birthday with my yearly $30 coupon. I loved Benihana, it's such a happy place. But once I received that voicemail from my sister calling to share the news of my daddy, every part of me shattered eternally. I was experiencing another loss.

On my ride home from Benihana, my friend decided to play Jhene Aiko's song "W.A.Y.S.." I knew my friend's intentions were good, but there's something about a sad song that makes the pain feel 10x worse and she kept freaking playing it! Damn, it's like the artist is expressing your pain through a song for you. Especially if the lyrics speak to your current experience and they did.

"I gotta keep going. I gotta keep going. I gotta keep going. I gotta show them that I could keep going."

Jhene sang with so much compassion and with such an angelic voice that tore more and more at my heart! "Ahhhh Daddy!" (silently cries).

Later that day I made my way to my daddy's house. I immediately ran up the stairs to find him resting there. There's a lot I want to hold sacred for us in our last moments so I won't share, but I'd never thanked God enough for allowing me to be there with my daddy in his last moments. I held on to his hand. I laughed. I cried. I reminisced. I forgave. I acknowledged his efforts as a human being and as a man! I praised his heroism as a leader, a father, someone who'd become my best friend. I wished peace for him and anything that had ever mattered to him. I prayed that he would be free. I prayed that he would not be scared, that we would not be scared.

Fortunately, both my brothers were able to have phone time from prison and got the opportunity to connect with our dad in his last moments. That was also one of the hardest things I had to do. I had to witness our dad say goodbye while knowing my brothers could not be there with him, knowing that there was no one to hug my brothers in that moment of loss.

In that moment I thanked God that He provided the opportunity to at least hear comfort in their voices. I couldn't imagine the thoughts in their heads and hearts (as father and sons), being that they would not get to physically connect before my daddy's departure from earth. I still can't imagine what they would have said if given the time and space to say more, or to be more vulnerable, or to simply be there. Brothers, if I never told you before ... I kissed daddy for you and held his hand so tight for you. He loved you both so much.

I was told that in the Islamic religion it is highly encouraged that you don't weep over someone's body as it is preparing to transition into another realm. I so desperately wanted to ignore every part of the advice, but I respected my daddy, I know his love for Allah was real. I held my composure and continued to embrace our last sacred moments together tear-free but with a heart full of tears.

By Monday, I was hopeful that God would return and restore every ounce of energy into my daddy's body and spirit, but God had other plans. Our last moments were something out of a movie that I will also hold sacred. You would really have had to be there to understand how it was to witness his last moments here on this earth.

What I took out of his last moments was that God was real, my daddy was at peace, and that he was surrounded by love. I thought to myself, what a way to transition, in pain but at peace. He looked so good and angelic to me. Yes, daddy you still looked good.

His demise is something that I have yet to come to peace with. Eight years have passed, and I still have heavy and deep feelings that sometimes come and go, and sometimes linger for a while. I often experience feelings of hurt mixed with curiosity. We had so much life to live together. I also have feelings of resentment because I felt the judicial system robbed us of so much of our time together. I then feel sadness that he is not here to witness the legacy he has created with his grandkids and great grandkids. I once felt confused but as I mature, I have learned that from Allah (God) we come and to Allah (God) we shall return.

I laugh at the fact that my brothers and I still don't know what we are mixed with. We never got a chance to get an answer to that question from our father. Honestly, the younger girl and the grown woman in me have so many questions and memories that I wanted to create during this lifetime. Those opportunities have ceased.

I was by my daddy's side from the moment he took his last breath until he was buried; dust to dust literally. Unfortunately, due to both of my brother's incarceration they were unable to physically be present. That for sure added insult to injury. I personally feel that individuals who are incarcerated should be able to pay respect to their loved ones on the outside who transition. I also believe there should be an emergency visitation in place for when someone is grieving the loss of life. The indecency to provide no support, no space to grieve, just an empty four walls that echoe your cries if you have any left in you, appears inhumane.

Omar was who I needed to see, and I needed to see him immediately. So, I scheduled a visit to his prison. Something about his tone of voice, his calmness, his spirit, his ability to look at the glass half full was what I needed in my moment of grief. I never asked him what he needed during his moment of grief, but I can guarantee we needed each other. I arrived at the visitation site sad, but that I did not show. I probably cried my whole two and a half hour drive there. My heart was heavy.

Per usual, the front desk people gave me havoc. For the first time I didn't fight back. My spirit was low, and there wasn't anything they could say or do to impact my mood more than it had been. Before my brother came out to visit, I got myself together fast. I straightened my hair, washed my face, guzzled some water, and tried to save face and enjoy the visit. We embraced each other in a hug for a while. Not as long as I desperately needed but enough to release the anxiety I had been feeling around seeing him after our daddy's return home to Allah.

I don't remember jumping right into conversation about it or even asking how he felt. It just was what it was, the pink elephant in the room. My brother has a way of lightening up the mood. He started to share stories about when he was a kid and how he was raised with our moms and pops (daddy). I laughed and sat back in amazement, learning things about a man I loved but never got a chance to deeply know. Omar's stories were parallel to the stories that the brothers at Unity Two, Black Panther Party Los Angeles, and the Nation of Islam shared during my daddy's celebration of life ceremony. So I knew his stories were true.

As my big brother talked, I could feel my tears forming. I begged myself not to cry and I didn't. My brother was a splitting image of my daddy. Their eyes, I swear their big brown hazel eyes share similarities. To the three wrinkled lines on each side of their face. The full thick eyebrows and their skin complexion. From the texture of their beard and hair, to the hair that grows out their ears. Oh, and God the way that they laugh. A genuine laugh followed with a courageous and contagious smile. I sat there like a kid in a candy store soaking up knowledge, trying to hold on to every word to feel connected to them both.

I had to leave that prison the same way I came. With a broken heart and without my big brother. They say the eyes are the windows to a person's soul. Please follow me, if you are truly a believer; I want you to know that during that day I held on to a vivid snapshot in my mind of my brother's eyes. Through his eyes I saw my daddy. Through his eyes is where I felt connected most.

I love you daddy, and YOU ARE ALWAYS WITH ME. Thank you for leaving the best part of you in each one of us. We are because you were.

- -

6-3-12—-Pops!

Brother Latif, Greetings Pop! Yeah its yo son extending mines with a strong, firm, iron grip. I had no idea you jumped ship and made it out of the shark tank. Allah willing you'll proceed down the righteous path. Pop I appreciate the concern and aid you give, but honestly I rather you focus on self, live life bro; and most of all put the time, energy, & focus on the kids. Sheeda literally desires/needs a father's presence and wants you in her life permanently. Yeah and bro could use your presence as well. I be worried about him based on I'm not 100% certain he can withstand everything that comes with this cesspool, especially if he swangs to these 4 yard 180 design. N E Ways I can tell someone gave some info about me being in low spirits based on your missile was aimed at me being strong :) HA HA HA. Yea pops I'm very aware of the heavy's you dropped on me. They're some inspirational political old heads. Pops this hole, shu's, & 4 yards are overrated and can't by any means fuck with me in no way. I'm hot because of the losses I take and $, visits, phone calls, etc. I'm sacrificing for an illusion "a cause that doesn't exist anymore" and my queens be hot & disappointed in my lack of judgment. My daughter hasn't even responded to my kites since I fell in this one, so yea a negro stressed semi by I counterattack that by beasting out on my routine exercising mind & body (everyday) so "Still I rise." Ill regardless of misfortunes I can't control. The euro committee said if I am cool back here they'll kick me out in a few months. Pops I'm starting to believe this just may be my destiny. These Euros don't even follow their own common law so me knowing their corrupt, soulless, racist asses I feel hopeless. I'm still going to fight based on I'm a fighter refusing to cave/ buckle to oppression and THE BIG BULLIE AMERIKKKANS! Yeah Baba I haven't received any funds but I'll be here so If it comes (cool) if not still (cool). I know your plate overrunneth with responsibilities so "do you."

Happy belated B'day. Yeah that's cold when you don't know your pops B'day. It just shows how dysfunctional we were in our past time. It's good we're both warriors knowing, understanding & accepting we're flawed but mean good. Pops you take care of yourself old dude. I can actually say I finally have major for you respect & love! Send mines to everyone. I'm outty 5000 4 now the oink oinks about to pick up mail so let me backup for now. Live life brother.. Leaving, how I entered "soldier'd up" <u>A STRONG CLENCHED FIST.</u>

LOVE, YO SON MM1

- -

6.3.12 — POPO!

BROTHER LATIF, GREETINGS POP! YEAH its YO SON extending mines with A STRONG, FIRM, irongrip. I HAD NO IDEAL YOU jumped SHIP AND MADE it OUT OF THE SHARKSTANK. ALLAH WILLING YOU'LL proceed DOWN THE RIGHTOUS PATH. POP i APPRECIATE THE CONCERN AND AID YOU give, but HONESTLY I RATHER YOU FOCUS ON SELF, live life BRO, AND MOST OF ALL put THE time, energy, & FOCUS ON THE Kids. SHEEDA literally desires/need A FATHER presence AND WANTS you in Her Life permantly. YEAH AND BRO could use your presence AS well. I be worried About HIM based on I'M not 100% certain He can withstand everything that comes with this cesspool, especially IF HE SWANGS to these 4 yard 180design. N.E.WAYS I CAN tell someone gave you some INFO about ME being on LOWspirits based on your missle was Aimed At me being strong :) HA HA HA YEAH POPS I'M VERY AWARE OF THE HEAVY's YOU dropped on me. THEY'RE some inspirational political old heads. POPS THIS HOLE, SHU's, & 4 yards are overratted and CAN'T by ANY means FUCK with me in NO way! I'M HOT because the losses I take $, visits, phonecalls, etc I'M SACRIFICING FOR A ILLUSION "A CAUSE THAT doesn't exsist anymore" AND MY QUEENS be HOT & disappointed in MY LACK OF JUDGEMENT. MY DAUGHTER HASN'T EVEN responded to MY Kites since I fell ON THIS ONE, SO YEAH A NEGRO STRESSED semi but

I counterattack that by beasting out on my routine exercising mind & body (everyday) so "still I rise" ill-regardless of misfortunes I can't control. The euro-committee said if I be cool back here they'll kick me out in a few months, Pops I'm starting to believe this just may be my destiny these euros don't even follow their own common law so me knowing their corrupt, soulless, racist asses I feel hopeless. I'm still going to fight based on I'm a fighter refusing to cave/buckle to oppression and the big bullie Amerikkkans. Yeah Baba I haven't received any funds but I'll be here so if it comes (cool) if not still (cool), I know your plate overrunnith with responsibilities so "do you".

Happy belated bday, yeah thats cold when you don't know your pops bday. It just shows how dysfunctional we were in our past time. It's good we're both warriors knowing, understanding, & accepting we're flawed but mean good. Pops you take care of yourself old dude, I can actually say I finally have majors for you respect & love / send mines to everyone, I'm outta sooo 4 now the oink oinks about to pick up mail so let me back up for now. Live life brother.. leaving how I entered "soilder'd up" a strong clenched fist

Love, yo son

MM

MOE

It took me days to start this process pertaining to my relationship with my father. Our relationship was minimal, so I experience a lot of mixed emotions when expressing my sentiments.

My father was the type who displayed tough love. I guess he felt my mom, aunty, grams, and granny gave me too much affection. So when we did spend time together, he made sure to counteract the nurturing I'd received by pushing his views and beliefs on me with an iron fist. He pressed all mandatory participation in sports, karate classes, Islamic practices, and higher learning. What made it land on deaf ears and made me finally rebel against his practices, was the fact he wasn't there for me or my mom.

I had to witness my mom often struggle to get me the bare necessities. By the young age of 12 or 13 I despised my father and had no respect for the man who helped give me life. My mom was so sweet, loyal, and real; she always pointed out the good in him to me. By this time, I was as crazy as O Dog from the classic film *Menace 2 Society*. So, my father was dead in my eyes.

I considered my father to be my uncle or my big relative. Those two were more present to guide and mold me as a boy, teen, and young man. When I got too wild in the streets or disrespectful with my mom, my uncles would be the one to scold me or discipline me with man blows. My father every blue moon tried to catch me on the corner of the block or in the trap house and give a few minutes of fatherly advice, but he saw and felt no respect from me towards him, so our relationship never developed.

As I grew behind these walls, I began to open my eyes as well as my soul. I needed to forgive all those I hated and despised, and my father was on the top of the list. When it came time to forgive him it felt as if a boulder was lifted off me, allowing me to let go of a childhood beef.

This man was highly educated and just wanted more for his son than what I was engaged in (gangs). His presence in my life as a man ignited the fire within me to study, learn, and find a platform, which produced a productive side of me. He sent authors, books, topics, literature, and advice to support my advancement. He knew from street talk, prison gossip, and his common sense that I pledged allegiance to a gang and was a decorated soldier building my way up in the ranks. He finally conceded to my choice but still implied that I was front line for a "bigger cause" like fighting for our people. We would now talk, laugh, clown, and appreciate our relationship even though it came 20 years later under lock and key. I was born into struggle so to finally receive a love that was lost amidst my coldest struggle was priceless, rewarding, and I was thankful.

Losing my father under these circumstances just added to the fury I hold against the system. My sisters took it the hardest, and to not be there to console them was heartbreaking. Now all kinds of thoughts come into my mind, questions, and emotions I didn't think existed. Love, loss, and life are crazy like that.

My father was a ladies' man, intelligent, a leader, a loner, a humorous individual. He'd give his last to anyone, he didn't base his interactions with people on what they had or didn't have. He was point blank a Black Panther, always for the people. His smile was infectious, but he'd turn serious in a second if need be. I see myself in him "good, bad, and ugly." Now I laugh but I wish we could laugh together.

My sister and I would like to know what other blood we possess aside from African. My father's genetics and features are strong. We believe we have Middle Eastern in us, or at least I do. I've been told we have Cherokee (Indian) blood within us as well. It matters only to a degree because when the smoke clears, my roots, beliefs, and love are dedicated to the African movement.

My father and I seem to have had the same taste in women. Most men's attraction comes from a woman's outer beauty which is relatable, but I feel that is vague. I am attracted to a woman's strength, character, and intellect. I love a confident woman but if she is too vain, I'll pass because she'll end up getting clowned.

My father's last wife is a Black queen. I respect that she is very hands-on with teaching, supporting, and utilizing her wisdom to educate others. She mobilizes for the people who are incarcerated and spiritually broken from harsh realities. She's part of a program that focuses on the healing of women of incarcerated family members – specifically sisters, moms, grams, or wives. It's a group that holds meetings, attends court dates, and mobilizes prison visits, etc. The fruit doesn't fall far from the tree, so I knew I would end up with a woman who has passion for a similar cause.

As I lay on my metal rack a million thoughts cross my mind. My body is in bondage, but they can't enslave my mind. I've tried to master becoming spiritually free and thinking positively, hoping to ignite positive results.

Every day, minute, hour, and moment are challenging and breathtaking. To live behind the wall as someone with a life sentence, on a 180-Level IV yard for over 20 years, can't be measured or explained in words. You lose yourself and find yourself, it's an emotional and mental roller coaster.

This weekend I was looking out my back window. There's no view of grassland, lakes, animals, mountains, city, citizens, etc., but in my building I have a view of visitors coming and going. The visiting room is in eyesight. As I paced my cage, I happened to be listening to R&B music. I tripped off the 80 % of Latino families arriving – elders, kids, and wives – compared to the 20% ratio of Black families coming to visit their loved ones. It was a sad sight and ugly realization.

I can't clown the sisters for not making these trips especially when I am conscious of the many obstacles that stand in their way. My sister and I had a dialogue about it and of course she defended her Black Queens saying we brothers expect a sister to run for us. We want to be players, pimps, and gangsters who have multiple women but can't give back the time, energy, loyalty, and sacrifice we expect.

Personally, I respect the Black Queen and can only see myself married to a Black gem. The sister knows my struggle, plight, and opposition because she's one in me. To each its own but a lot of brothers are crossing over to White woman; I see them on the TV, in the videos, and at visiting and I just want to be like "wow never me." I guess it's like father, like son because pops never had a White woman, it just wasn't our thing. As an inmate we must get it where we live so the survival skills are reciprocated. I am just an advocate of Black Love. I'd love to see us with each other.

This book is developed by a brother and sister who haven't allowed the slave chains, system, odds, or negative energy in general to shake, rattle, break or deter our bond and love for one another. We're under attack on every level (Blacks), and we make it easy to be snuffed out by having self-hate, being ignorant and misinformed, or just not caring about reform whether it's in here or out there.

You can be a prisoner in society if you have a narrow mind or have chains on your mind. We must learn to expand our mind by doing big, dreaming big, and reaching big. It's all about the company you keep that'll support your growth or keep you stagnated with the low-level have-nots.

I've always been eager to learn and always wanted better things in life, so being content with what I've shown the world so far hasn't been an option. My sister, mom, and a handful of women have been pivotal in opening my eyes to making positivity a way of life; how I act, how I think, and how I respond. It's a cold test daily; I'm so accustomed to lashing out, being mentally and physically destructive, or just allowing negativity to win out over reform.

When one has given over 30 years to a negative lifestyle, change doesn't occur overnight. Sometimes I feel as if my mom and sister want a better life for me and love me more than I do myself. They have never left my side amidst the struggles I've battled with endlessly.

A support system is vital with doing time, you go through mental adjustment daily. This place is literally a zoo, a warehouse, a slave plantation; the effect it has on the human soul is unexplainable. It can break the strongest person mentally, physically, emotionally, and spiritually. You need a reminder that you matter, you're worth loving, visiting, and sacrificing for.

Imagine the million souls who are without support. They adopt prison ways and constitutions which will give them the support needed. A void must be filled to withstand living a life behind these soulless walls. I'm blessed in many ways, and I never take it for granted that my mind is sharp, I'm a spiritual being in tune with my Lord and savior, my emotions are in check, and physically I'm mobile and still marching like a trooper, despite my false imprisonment.

Since my father's departure from this earth, I've pondered taking my Shahada to convert to Islam. I feel more comfortable praying with my people; the have nots, the oppressed, the ghetto children who still rise up – strong-minded, strong-willed, Black and proud with dignity about ourselves. The ones who know their history and are proud of their birthplace regardless of the slave chains we wear. Whether I convert or not, I'll still push my father's agenda based on his views that I've inherited. I'm a Black Panther and revolutionary with a red flag uniform.

Thanks pops.

11-4-12

Pops this will be a brief but concise missile. As you know my seed has fallen victim to these oppressed enclaves. Yea I'm guilt stricken since I take responsibility for her actions. Also last time I wrote I was going through a reality check. Moms had just gone through an operation (Allah blessed me) with it being a success. But the lesson learned was I can't accept losing my mom from behind these enemy lines. Sheeda has too much on her plate. She's sacrificing her time, movement, $, companionship, traveling, & desires to look after me, bro, & moms. It kills me! I've told her to let me be. I can stand the rain "struggles" shit I'm not like these soft (cotton candy negros) who melt/cry with the sight of rain. Pop (real talk) as men bro, let me know when something is foul amidst our fam. I know mom & sis worry about my reactions but I'm eventually going to find out & deal with it. N-E Ways I'm in Ad-Seg now (Post-Shu). I'm just awaiting my bus ticket to Kern Valley or back to Salinas. Wherever I plant my boots I'm on a mission. Pa we can't let no one impede our push with the lawyer. . Boy needs to know a soldier means bizzness! We'll talk later over the horn in details. Tell your wifey I send mines in full and as soon as I get situated I'll address her last missile "She's Real"! Well pops don't overwork them old bones :) We need you around. Also I'm so through with that slave name (Jones) I want to certify another handle like Omar Latif Abdul. Feel Me? I'll Hollar! M-M1

Ps: I've ran through all the innocence projects but I appreciate you trying all avenues.

11.4.12

pop this will be a brief but concise missle. As you know my seed has fell victim to thee oppressed enclave, yeah I'm guilt stricken since I take responsibility for her actions. Also last time I wrote I was going through a reality check, [redacted] had just went through an operation "Allah blessed me" with it being a success. But the lesson learned was I can't except losing my mom from behind these enemie lines. Sheeda has to much on her plate she's sacrifising her time, movement, $, companionship, traveling, & desires to look after me, bro & moms. It kills me / I've told her to let me be. I can stand the rain "struggles" shit I'm not like these soft (cotton candy negros) who melt/cry with the sight of rain. Pop (real talk) as men bro, let me know when somethings afoul amidst our fam, I know mom & sis worry about my reactions but I'm eventually going to find out & deal with it. N.E.ways I'm in Ad-Seg now (post-SHU) I'm just awaiting my bus ticket to Kern Valley or back to Salinas. Where ever I plant my boots I'm on a mission. PA we can't let curt impede our push with the lawyer. [redacted]

[redacted]. Boy needs to know a soldier means bizzness! We'll talk over the horn in details. Tell [redacted] I send mines in full and soon as I get situated I'll address her last missle. "She's real"! Well pops don't overwork →

them old bones ☺ we need you around. Also I'm so through with that slave name (Jones) I want to certify another handle like Omar Latif Abdul. Feel me? I'll holla!

PS: I've ran through all the innocent project but I appreciate you trying all avenues

CHAPTER 8: FACE THE WORLD – 20 YEARS LATER

RASHEEDA

If you are spiritual and a believer in a higher power and/or believe in the law of attraction, then you will say "God has a funny way of showing you things."

I believe that to be true.

It was winter of 2017 when I learned of a famous ABC network show called *Blackish* starring Tracey Ellis Ross and Anthony Anderson, written by Kenya Barris, a Clark Atlanta University Alumni. In the show they addressed race and mass incarceration in such a powerful way.

The episode titled "Please Don't Feed the Animals" explored mass incarceration it's impact, the stigma around individuals incarcerated, and how the odds are stacked against them post-release from prison. I'm not a fan of television because of the ongoing rhetoric, stereotypes, and propaganda they constantly push as an agenda, but this episode was brilliant. It not only educated and informed a wide audience on a major network, but it touched my core.

One of the characters in this episode was incarcerated and fighting for his innocence. The character's name just so happened to be Omar! I immediately was intrigued yet triggered. A part of me was so grateful that the creators were shedding light to my everyday reality, but I was also triggered that what I was watching was my everyday reality.

In one scene Anthony Anderson's character "Dre" and Tracey Ellis Ross' character "Bow" receive a call from their cousin Omar. The scene went like this:

"Bow: Dre, I just got the best news. Omar just called. The innocence project stepped in. He is innocent!

Dre: Wait, what?

Bow: He is getting out!

Dre: Out?

Bow: Yes!

Dre: From jail?

Bow: Yes!

Dre: Omar?

Bow: Yes, Dre! They are letting him out, and he – he's gonna get his life back.

Dre: Look at God."

In the scene Bow showed great excitement, enthusiasm, and joy while Dre displayed disbelief. He could not believe what he was hearing. As for me, I shed tears after that scene. I literally hopped out of my bed to rewind what I knew my eyes just witnessed and my heart needed to hear.

I played the scene back at least five times before I recorded it and shared it with my family and social media friends. Although I cried initially, my heart smiled every time I rewatched the scene with Bow sharing proudly "Omar is coming home."

That was music to my ears and a different sense of joy. It was the law of attraction and God's way of showing us signs. In real life, Omar is coming home!

Even though I'd been in many courtrooms since my brother's guilty verdict was read in 1999 it always gave me anxiety when I entered one. I'd watched people I loved endure similar battles in court proceedings and it always reminded me of my experience as a child.

My personal experiences within the judicial system are the reasons I had wanted to become a lawyer. Yes, initially growing up I thought I could win battles in a courtroom by becoming a lawyer – and If I could become a lawyer, I could get my brother free. But after investing time and sacrificing money to some of the best lawyers in Los Angeles (including a famous lawyer who was once Michael Jackson's attorney), I would always sense a feeling of defeat. If they can't get my brother home, then can I as a lawyer? That thought always lingered.

In 2017, we got the news! It was some of the most hopeful news we'd received in a while, and it was surely a testament of faith and long years of deep prayer and discussion with God. Omar had been granted another hearing for his case. This was what the family had been waiting for over 20 years. This was the moment that I knew my brother had always fantasized about, "getting justice" for all the time that had been stolen.

Here we were mid-week arriving back at the Los Angeles Superior Court. This time around there were no long lines or a big rush of people, so the process to enter felt seamless.

Although I was anxious, I took my time. I was in no rush to meet the judge. I laid my small purse on the conveyor, removed my keys from my pockets as I walked through the metal detector. I greeted the security guards and on que, grabbed my personal items from the conveyor belt and walked to the elevators.

Law enforcement, security, lawyers, and strangers all smiled as they engaged with each other. Suit and ties, and respective uniforms all felt like they belonged. I observed for a minute, mindful of my energy but also still anxious in hope that all would go well for Omar.

As I exited the elevator, I noticed familiar faces. My mom, my maternal uncle, my twin brother's significant other, my aunt, and a host of people were all there in support of my brother and his hearing. I paid close attention to my mom as we hugged and embraced each other with love. As I hugged her, I needed her to feel my energy. I needed her to know we were all here together and that what she experienced 20-something years ago would not happen again.

As a woman now, I had the ability to hold my mom and be the strength she needed for whatever the outcome would be for my brother. I posted my last Instagram post, our family said a prayer, and the court proceeding started.

I will never forget the name of the person who was the presiding judge over my brother's hearing. This was the man who ultimately held the keys to his freedom during this proceeding. His name stuck to my memory like a magnet because I knew that this time around there were no jurors. The decision was based on the power of one person. We watched my brother be escorted from the back by a sheriff. Omar walked in draped in a Dodger blue LA County Jail jumpsuit with a pair of black Bob Barker shoes.

It was nothing new that he was shackled in chains and handcuffs. His hands were cuffed in front of his waist, with another pair of metal cuffs on his ankles. A king to us but a slave to them. I know that the security procedure consists of individuals being shackled in metal handcuffs, to prevent a physical attack or an escape from police custody – but this was a human being who was coming to "ask for freedom." I think less chains would have sufficed.

As he walked in, we were all just so happy as a family to see Omar healthy, happy, and hopeful in the flesh. For my aunt and uncle, it was joyful as they had not seen him in person in two decades because of the visitation restrictions. For some people it was their first time putting a face to Omar as they'd only heard stories of him and were there for moral support. As a family and community, we wanted my brother home, we needed him home.

During the court proceeding I tried to remain calm as I sat in my seat listening to all the legal jargon being tossed around. I understood some of the dialogue being used in court, but some stuff I lacked knowledge or any understanding of. My ears hung onto the negative verbiage being used against Omar, but I couldn't understand why at an evidence hearing his character at 19 or his prison disciplinary record was relevant?

I am not making light of any matter or situation, but I believe in sticking to facts. "Omar Jones" is not guilty of the crime that he has been serving all this time for, regardless of what he has done while trying to survive in a place like prison.

As court continued, I wondered what was on his mind? What was he feeling? If he could make any moment in time stand still, what would it be? Those were my thoughts. Just the opportunity to get back to the superior court was a monumental moment for all of us and all we wanted was to be victorious in this matter.

Three days of court proceedings continued . . . . . .

On the last day, you could hear the lint fall from one's clothes onto the floor. That is how quiet the courtroom was. Nobody had much to say. We prayed and we walked in faith that Omar was coming home.

Were we prepared financially? No. We probably were not prepared mentally but physically we could not wait to welcome him with the love we longed for with big hugs, deep kisses, and a warm embrace. The judge, who I will never forget, gave us exactly what we did not want. The judge decided that he would not give my brother freedom.

There was a loss of words, loss of thoughts, and blank stares on the faces of supporters who'd come to show solidarity. For the first time in a long time, no one had anything to say. What could we really say? It was Omar who was going back.

As a family we'd been waiting for this opportunity and the outcome was not what we'd prayed for. There had been never-ending prayers, car washes to raise funds, and selling plates of food just to help Omar get another chance.

They say don't question God, so I did not. I have yet to come to Him with a question of why, but I do want to know when; when will this experience be put to rest for all those attached, invested, and impacted?

Everyone went to their respective places to grieve as they saw fit, whether that was alone or together. For me, I went to eat and take a nap. So much energy had been consumed in how everyone would feel, and I knew I needed to just rest. I wasn't sure what the next step in this battle would consist of, but I knew that I had to write about it.

That day I made up my mind and heart that after Omar was sent back to prison, I would continue to evolve as a woman, a sister, and a warrior who'd continue to be my brother's keeper. That I would continue to remain true, hopeful, faithful, and resilient. Reminding myself that a system would never break me, or the bond Omar and I shared.

I thought to myself, "Rasheeda, school is over, but you will forever be a student. You have grown through experiences over the years on a quest for purpose, owning her desires, and ultimately being a woman that is coming home to birth new goals and higher vibrations. Your brothers may or may not be there when you buy your first home, for your wedding, baby shower, or moments that are special to you. Although it brings deep pain, you will be okay. Remain steadfast. Continue to grow, transform, and make everywhere you go a home. God welcomed you back to Los Angeles, back to the palm trees to fulfill the footprints left by your ancestors. For every tear dropped you better make life worth it. May your fight for justice become personal for your brothers, but ultimately, please start with yourself."

Even though Omar hadn't come home with us just yet, I didn't know what words I would say to him when he got the chance to call. We did not know who he would call first, my mommy, his girlfriend at the time, or if he would be open or cared to talk to any of us. Although I had no new uplifting words to share, now was certainly not the time to sit with our heads down. I am not surprised that he called me first. He really does have a special place in his heart for me.

I remember him being very calm and saying something along the lines of "They really don't want me to come huh?!"

I sat with that statement for a second before I boasted with energy, "We should write a book!"

Thinking back, it sounds insensitive considering the space we were in, but it was the first thing that came to mind for whatever it was worth. I didn't have any tricks or shortcuts to life, but I found so much solace in writing. Writing had been my go to when I was up or down, so offering this to my brother in his time of suffering felt right.

Rather than allow this moment to defeat us, I suggested we write a book about our lives and the way incarceration has impacted us. With no hesitancy in his voice whatsoever, he responded with a yes. He was excited about the idea of turning his pain into purpose and it relieved me that he was open to the idea. I could only hope my brother found the same peace I had in writing, but more than anything, he could truly share his story and truth.

As Omar went to his cell to write what has blossomed into this body of work, I went on to redefine myself in a different scenery other than home, seeing that I had the liberty to do so. I was going on vacation, a real vacation.

The Vacation

This was my first getaway since learning that we'd have to fight harder than before to bring Omar home. I'd initially felt reluctant going on this trip, but I knew I needed to free my mind. As I made the conscious decision to not give up I still hurt but I couldn't mope around. I needed to reassure myself in every sense that when we rise in anything, we win.

The courts had given me confirmation with their verdict that I needed to find my smile again. My good friend and I planned a trip together. Usually when we plan our vacations, we first ask ourselves what our intentions are before selecting the location. The space we are in mentally, emotionally, and financially determines where we go.

She knew I needed a vacation because of all that I'd experienced so she allowed me to take the lead on this one. I knew I needed to get away to refresh my magnetic energy and internal peace, but I did not know where. Where could I feel free and most liberated? Where could I connect with genuine people who wouldn't care what I have or where I come from, but only meet me with love?

My choice of adventure was very random to others, but intentional for me and a choice that I knew would serve me well. My dear friend/travel partner and I went back and forth for a while due to some minor casualties, but landed in the beautiful country of Haiti.

Haiti was not only beautiful because of the people, scenic feel, and the food, but also because it was a country that provided a haven for all formerly enslaved people. I was traveling to the first Black independent country, and to me that was powerful. I did not know what to expect but I was advised to be extra cautious and safe because of what the media shared. After falling in love in South Africa, Cuba, and Ghana I was starting to fall in love with culture and experiences outside of the states.

Arriving at the place I'd call home while in Haiti was breathtaking. After setting my luggage down, I took time to digest and be in pure gratitude for all that was around me. We rented out an Airbnb that was designed as a beach house.

The beach house was surrounded with palm trees, water, and dirt roads. The house had no windows, shades, or screens so it allowed the wind and sun to penetrate the floor plan while providing the opportunity to overlook all that God created. The blue water and sunshine were far better than Los Angeles could provide at the time. I was fortunate, delighted, and was in solitude away from home.

Okay, would you believe me if I said that my friend missed her flight? Yes, my good sister missed her flight which led me to be in Haiti alone for a day and a half. Initially, I was bummed as I was in a foreign country alone. Not only was I bummed to be alone, but for the first couple hours I was really scared.

If you have ever been abroad, you know that there is a high possibility that the power can go out depending on where you are. There was a moment where I didn't have power or window seals, and all I had to my name was a laptop for light and my pepper spray. However, after a couple deep breaths, a prayer to God, and faith that I would be okay, the generous property manager ensured my safety and provided me with a generator to restore the power. The light and safety reassurance allowed me to accept the fact that there was nothing I could do but wait and make the most of my time alone until my friend arrived.

I figured I would make the most of my time by doing something that was relaxing and meaningful. I had already journaled about my experience and gone through some of my favorite songs, so I decided to grab the book, *The Alchemist*, that I had been wanting to read. A friend of mine had recommended this book to me, knowing I was a lover of good reads. I'd started it and stopped, then started again due to distractions. But once I started reading it again, I was glued in.

I loved how the message in the book was about discovering one's destiny (personal legend) and never losing faith. If there was ever a perfect time to read this book, it was now, here in Haiti.

Going back to how funny life can be sometimes, I had already affirmed that I wanted to continue to discover my purpose, and here I was in solitude on day one with the opportunity to reflect, read, and enjoy this time alone. I went from being scared, hating the fact my friend had missed her flight, to getting lost in this book on a journey with this character Santiago.

Santiago's story in *The Alchemist* was inspiring. It allowed me to see how faith and meeting people along your journey in life matters. I pinned the book after a couple chapters in and decided to get some rest. I was tired.

The next day, I was eager to explore and looked forward to enjoying the outdoors of Jacmel, Haiti. I didn't have any plans because I hadn't thought I'd be alone, so I figured I'd ride around town and live in the moment. I decided to take an impromptu tour so I could see the coast.

I reconnected with my taxi (motorcycle) driver, a Haitian man who gave me an authentic and genuine experience. He had smooth dark skin, nice-length locks, a contagious smile, and a deep Haitian accent that I could barely understand, but I trusted that he would ensure my safety. His demeanor was cool, calm, and relaxing, and to my surprise even though I was currently alone, I was at ease. He told me to hop on his bike and I saddled on the back of the Moto-concho, wrapping my arms around him as we sat to ride off into the sunset.

Have you ever taken a deep sigh of relief for whatever reason and felt relaxed? Relieved from all things, well that's kind of how I felt. As we rode, I gracefully admired Haiti and the beauty that we don't hear much about.

Haiti is a very beautiful place, even though it's labeled one of the poorest countries. I admired the Black people of different descents, yet from the same creation. I sat on the back of the bike, holding onto him and all I could think of aside from the amazing view, was the word 'maktub'.

During my reading of *The Alchemist* it was described that while on his journey, Santiago learns of the concept 'maktub', meaning "it is written." 'Maktub' exemplifies the idea that some things are meant to be. The concept becomes the theme of Santiago's adventures and relationships throughout the book. Here I was in my own adventure, feeling like Santiago.

Like Santiago, I came to realize, "Rasheeda, it is written. You are here for a reason, and everything is happening as it should."

I didn't hold any doubts along my tour ride, as we moved up and down the coast. I knew my mom would hate the idea of it, and true enough it was not the wisest idea to trust a stranger in foreign land, but God was with me. I felt liberated. For a moment on the ride, I wished that both my brothers would one day too feel the same sense of liberation that I felt. I had a moment of sadness while riding but those feelings were short-lived in knowing they would indeed experience this freedom, and until then I would feel it for them.

We rode around the country for at least an hour, coasting along the highway as the weather was perfect. There was a nice breeze that brushed past me, but it wasn't cold. The streets weren't too busy and when they were, I still felt free. I hadn't known this Haitian man before that day, but the experience is something I always go back to because it was a moment where I felt the most free.

There were limited cars on the road and seemed as if the path had been cleared just for us. I closed my eyes and took in the moment. I opened my eyes from this euphoric moment only to see his locks and my braids continuing to blow through the breeze. I smiled at the joy of peace, mesmerized by the sight of all that was observed on the journey.

You'd think this was a fairytale moment, but nope, without a doubt this was my reality. There's this assumption, a beautiful life can't be lived for whatever reason during suffering, but life can and will be whatever it is you make it to be.

Is life hard? Absolutely, but it must be lived. As Santiago lived his life to find his personal legend (purpose) I knew that freeing Omar would always be an obligation and priority in my life, even if/when that changes. What better place to come to this realization, than in a place that is rooted in liberation?

When I returned from Haiti, I had emotionally broken down maybe once. I felt like I was surrounded by so much love, but no one understood me. The pain and burden of having a loved one incarcerated was a beast in disguise. It was like a roller coaster ride that you begged to finish before it even began. I felt it was the most honorable yet loneliest experience to be so dedicated and loyal to one's freedom and life.

I shared my general feelings and thoughts with one of my friends. Holding the weight was heavy and I could no longer bear it. However, the hesitancy to share and be vulnerable about "jail" and my experience with it showed up again.

I think I felt hesitant because no matter how much I expressed using my words, no one could ever really understand how it feels unless they've lived the experience themselves. It's like being Black; being a part of an experience and a culture of something you just can't describe.

To say the least, I gained some courage and shared my feelings. As I was sharing with my friends one of them expressed "You are so brave."

Another friend said, "You are resilient as f*ck."

One of my newest friends who didn't know much about my past life said, "Hey friend, I thought you were being dramatic about your life." At that moment I knew she'd never really heard me, but that day she had some insight as to why I go so hard in work, in love, in family, and the fight for freedom and equality. She was new to me and was just barely scratching the surface of what life had been for me, but her acknowledgement was a start.

"Naw this is my life and it's real."

I felt good sharing with her, but it still did not empower me to live in the truth of what it was like. I was tired of isolating myself. I needed to continue to explore ways to be free and seen.

Travel Continued

The same sense of joy and confirmation I felt when I watched the *Blackish* episode was the same confirmation I felt when going on vacation to the motherland, to visit the beautiful Lagos, Nigeria.

I was flying on British Airways. British Airways is staffed with people from other countries besides the United States, at least this crew. If you've ever flown British Airways, you notice the lack of diversity, and oftentimes the way you are treated shows. But this experience was different. I didn't get an extra pillow when I asked. I for sure rang the bell 10 times, but each time I asked the wait grew longer. I eventually asked for another flight attendant to support me, especially seeing that I'd spent good money on my voyage.

The next lady who assisted me was sent from heaven. She was nice, welcoming, and she saw me – not just my need for extra pillows or Biscoff cookies, but she wanted to know more about my shirt which read "Justice for Omar."

"What happened to Omar?" she asked.

I paused for a second to gather my thoughts as to how I would respond. Would I give her the story from start to end? Give it to her brief about Omar, where he is, and the hope for his future? Or would I generalize Omar and share about how he's one of the million Black men in the United States who the judicial system has failed. I wanted to highlight his innocence above everything. If I had the capacity, I probably would have dissected all three, but I had to use the restroom, both of our languages created barriers for understanding, and the turbulence had me anxious. So, I spoke from the heart with sincerity as brief as I could.

"Omar is my brother. He was found guilty at 21 years old for a crime he did not commit. He has spent the last 22 years of his life in prison, a lot of the time in solitary confinement. Every day we fight for his innocence, praying that he comes home."

I instantly dropped my head as I could sense the tears coming. I lied, every day we didn't fight. But we should have.

Brother, I am sorry.

"That is so sad," her face read how she felt. She wore a look of disgust on her face and kept saying, "I am so sorry."

I nodded my head to her and smiled as I headed back to my seat releasing all the anxiety I was feeling. I always feel anxious when I tell the story because it requires reliving the experience again. It also just takes one person knowing the impact of incarceration and the need to dismantle the system. 10 minutes later I was given extra blankets and some cookies. I smiled, "presidential style" I said in my head. I was excited to be on this voyage of new experiences, but feelings of guilt from leaving my brothers behind remained.

We finally landed in our layover in the United Kingdom, and I was eager to run to the nearest exit. As I was exiting an attendee on the flight grabbed my arm. Now this is unfamiliar territory, I thought "Lady I am not going to take this blanket!"

But to my surprise she said, "I heard what happened to Omar. Good luck."

If I wasn't so tired from jet lag and in my right state of mind, I would have signaled to my eyes and released what I always feel but never get to express.

"Brother, they see you! They care to know. They send their best of wishes." I bowed my head and embraced her with a hug and told her "Thank you!"

(Rasheeda, next time cry. It is okay to cry).

Baggage claim was the next stop. "I just want to be in Nigeria already," I thought.

I was extremely overwhelmed by the process in Heathrow, but also overjoyed with the amount of attention I was receiving. It was like I was on *The Real Housewives of Atlanta*, or something similar.

As we were going through security people stopped us.

"Aye what happened to Omar?" a young male security asked.

I word for word repeated the same story I had told hours prior.

"Omar is my brother. He was found guilty at 21 years old for a crime he did not commit. He has spent the last 22 years of his life in prison, a lot of the time in solitary confinement. Every day we fight for his innocence."

As I continued to walk through the metal detector the airport security continued, "I heard they just released 600 innocent people in the states so good luck."

The states. That's what other countries call the United States, 'the states'. I hadn't heard that news but his message was meant for me to hear. Several other people I noticed glanced at my shirt that I'd worn for the past 24 hours. Whether they stopped and asked me, or their face just read out of general curiosity, I appreciated that my brother Omar had been seen.

Essie Justice

My father's wife introduced me to an organization called Essie Justice Group. She recommended that it would be worth my time to become familiar with the organization. Because of my love, admiration, and appreciation for her as my bonus mom, it was imperative that I gave the group a chance.

My stepmother was raw, real, and a revolutionary woman. She was much like my father; well spoken, beautiful, knowledgeable, and wise. Because I was on a quest for liberation, I trusted that Essie Justice Group would be good.

Essie Justice Group is a nonprofit organization of women with incarcerated loved ones taking on the rampant injustices created by mass incarceration. The Healing to Advocacy Program is a nine-week program where women impacted by incarceration break isolation by learning to advocate for themselves, their families, and community.

I went into my first Healing to Advocacy session open-minded, but also very hesitant, reserved, and naturally claimed to my own comfort. I didn't know what to expect when attending this group, I hadn't the slightest idea what I was walking into but again, I trusted her.

There was a group of about 10 women of different backgrounds and walks of life that formed a centric circle. These were women from all different professions, religions, socio-economic statuses, etc. who all shared one thing in common – we were women impacted by incarceration.

Here sat a group of women that understood me in ways a lot of my friends and others just couldn't understand. I don't say that in a negative way, because I genuinely love all my friends and I know they love me, but still I had felt a disconnect since I was a young girl.

Society has created a false narrative of what success looks like, what beauty looks like, and how one should live. Being honest with myself, this has hindered me internally while still allowing me to smile and cheer on the outside. Have you found yourself living life trying to create smiles and please everyone else, that you lose sight of your own pleasure at times? I think we all may have experienced feeling hidden, even while standing in the light. Well, this group of women helped me in ways I didn't think they would.

These same women fought a cause that I too cared about, and a fight that connected me to my family, friends, and my city. The more comfortable I became around these women, the more open I became.

Thinking back, there was one activity that we engaged in as a group during our nine-week program. The activity required that we face one member in our group to speak to for five minutes about ourselves, as our partner listened. For five minutes I had to share what came to mind first. This was the most vulnerable I had ever been in my life, especially to someone I barely knew.

During the five minutes I talked about my love for travel, my passion for education, my love for community, and my love for adventure. Three minutes into the activity I got deeper. I began to talk about my need for my dad and my need for my brothers. I yearned for their presence, their constant voices, their knowledge, and their protection. I remember I started to cry. I talked about how I felt embarrassed as a kid and never wanted to share my story.

It felt like the more I talked the less heavy the weight on my shoulders felt. I cried some more and continued to talk about how much I needed my brothers to be free. I wanted that more than anything. When the buzzer rang indicating my five minutes was up, my partner had to reflect on what she had just heard me say.

My partner held my hand and began to speak life into me. I allowed her to grab my hand and we just embraced that moment together. Let me say that again, she spoke life into me. The words that she shared showed me more than anything, that she'd heard everything that I'd said and that she saw me for me. She heard the pain, the determination, the fight, and my ambition. She saw a young girl in me that was becoming a woman, and seeking healing from a system that had caused us similar damage.

After that five-minute buzzer rang again, we both wiped our tears and embraced each other with more hugs. I wonder if she knew that moments like the one we shared were the moments that keep me going. That was the moment I knew I was right where I needed to be.

I'd been on a mission of liberation, focus, and ultimately strengthening every area of my being. It was in this space with Essie I'd been able to openly speak about my feelings towards injustices, and share the side of myself that I'd always kept a mystery. I was bothered by the statistics governing the judicial system, and the very laws that hadn't been favorable for people of color. It was breathtaking simply being a part of this group, I felt at liberty to express my truth, in realizing "the system got us all f*cked up!" (Please excuse my French).

During this time, I gained a voice and the courage to speak against mass incarceration. As women we went from strangers to being sisters by the end of the program. Every rose has a plethora of thorns on the stem, yet it doesn't take away the sweet fragrance of a bright, red, beautiful rose.

Here, I realized that I'd been hiding my truths and who I was for a very long time. It was here, I accepted that life for me would be a challenge, but a challenge that was worth fighting. Here, I learned that I had to empower myself first before I could continue to pour into others. Here, I'd taken a vow that no matter what the circumstances were, I'd empower all women to live in their truth. Now that I'd made this vow it was time for therapy to take my healing to new levels.

"I am what time, circumstance, history, have made of me, certainly, but I am also, much more than that."

–James Baldwin

Therapy

As I faced the world in quest of my brother's freedom, I knew it was important to educate, liberate, but most importantly heal myself if this was a fight I was going to continue. Now more than ever I was vocal about a lot of things I'd dealt with or faced.

There had been layers of Rasheeda I hadn't cared to share; whether it was out of self-doubt, feeling misunderstood, or not being provided the space to be vulnerable enough to share the things that might not have been as pretty. See, I found myself hiding certain personal things because society made me feel uncomfortable with my reality, but after pledging with Essie Justice, I found myself seeking more help.

Having experienced a break-up with "Superman", my brother's re-sentencing in court, recurrent trauma of grief and loss, on top of daily living and survival and all the joys and woes of becoming a woman, I needed a place to process all of it. I searched high and low for someone who wouldn't know me from a can of paint, someone who wasn't biased, and someone to help me help myself.

It was difficult finding a therapist that catered to my needs. I knew exactly what I needed my therapist to be for me, so I was picky in my process. I was once advised by a trusting supervisor when searching for a therapist to be specific with what you want or who you feel most comfortable with. My therapist needed to be a man. My therapist needed to be Black and needed to have certain experiences and possess a certain aura and energy. I could not risk for my secrets and vulnerable heart to be compromised again. After months of searching and one good conversation with a friend, I was referred to a Black male therapist also known to me as "the perfect match."

"What brings you in?" he asked.

I remember my first session with my therapist as I sat across from him in this small yet welcoming room. I sat with my legs crossed Indian style on his couch and he sat across in a stylish accent chair. I smiled anxiously and said that I was here to "process my traumas and experiences."

During my intake process I mentioned discussing my love interest and heartbreak to build rapport, but after several sessions of dialogue it was time to explore deeper levels of how life had impacted me. In each session we dove deeper into discussing my life up until my current age. In these sessions I grew wiser and more self-aware.

Session after session we explored my thoughts and feelings in real time about everything that mattered to me. I cried. I cried tears of joy and tears of sorrow but this time the tears were met with answers, reasoning, and questions that allowed me to reflect and look in the mirror at who I was and who I was becoming.

You see, my dad's incarceration subconsciously impacted me and so did my mom's, my uncles', my niece's, my cousins' and anyone else that I had to visit behind bars.

The loss and death of my friends and loved ones subconsciously made me feel anxious. The murder of countless friends and my relatives, Derek and Ramone, made me experience every symptom of PTSD every time I walked the neighborhood of South Central Los Angeles.

Anytime I would achieve or accomplish something it was always met with disappointment and guilt for those who could not physically be there to celebrate with me. All the feelings of sadness, grief, and fear were exposed but not judged, not even a little bit. I loved it here in this sacred space.

I smile thinking about how sometimes in therapy we laughed across the room. Most times I had the answers and knew what needed to be done all along, but I just needed to release and speak it aloud to myself and with a witness. Therapy reminded me that life had given me one hell of a deck of cards, and also reassured me that my resilience, optimism, hope, faith, and love would always see me through. God was using my therapist to speak to me, and although therapy was a pretty penny it was worth it.

After two years of meeting with my "perfect match" it was time to depart, based on the amount of growth that I'd displayed during our time together. There was something beautiful that transpired in this two-year relationship.

I was now able to identify my traumas, triggers, and develop ways to cope with things I had no control of changing. Some things were just the way they were, and I learned that that is okay.

I learned that even Superwoman sometimes needs to be more like Superman. I imagine there are days when Superman wakes up, glances over at his cape, and thinks when someone will come save him. Maybe my assignment here on earth was not to save everyone but just be a vessel in the ways that I can. In therapy I truly learned to save myself first and the rest will follow.

One of the last sessions I recall with my "perfect match" is when I acknowledged all the things that I'd been through and guess what, this time I didn't cry. I acknowledged that despite everything I was happy that I had still found reasons to smile. Life had not been that bad after all.

I made a gratitude list of all the many ways I'd been blessed; both tangible and intangible things i.e., breathing, friendships, my sanity, favor, etc. Some people cope with sex, drugs, relationships, and unhealthy things but there was a reason why God placed me around people, love, and situations for everything to make sense.

I thanked my "perfect match" more than enough during our last session. I smiled and laughed contagiously at the stories I'd shared throughout our time, thankful that he held a genuine, loving, and safe space for me. I ended our zoom session vowing that I would no longer hide behind my personal achievements and accomplishments.

I vowed that I would prioritize my mental health, self-care, and healing as a Black woman. I would no longer stay busy to avoid dealing with things that bothered me, and would embrace what I'd witnessed as a child, whether it was good, bad or indifferent. All those stories, memories, situations, and experiences helped shape who I was, who I am, and who I am becoming. I'm a proud daughter of my parents, and a descendant of the ancestors before me.

"The more you seek knowledge, the more one gains understanding. When you know better, you do better. But you must first know."

– Rasheeda Imani Jones

MOE

It was September of 2017 – 20 years of incarceration. I was housed in AdSeg pending an investigation after breaking institutional policies. I've been in the hole over 15 times throughout this prison bid; each episode has its own story as to reasons why. I'm a man of accountability nonetheless, but I've grown and matured from the boy I was.

One morning as me and my young homie were finishing up breakfast in our cell, we were interrupted by property officers approaching our cell door and announcing loudly, "Inmate Jones, roll your property, you're going to Men's Central Jail."

I'm thinking to myself, "Like who and for what?"

As if he could read my mind, he repeats the same sentence; instantly my adrenaline started to pump because I knew my writ of habeas corpus was under review.

A writ of habeas corpus orders the custodian of an individual in custody to produce the individual before the court, to make an inquiry concerning his or her detention.

This is what I'd hoped for since being removed from my family under false charges, but honestly after 20 years of continued denials, you start to subconsciously lose hope in humanity.

Reality set in, I wasted no time packing all my belongings. I recall informing my cellmate how good God is, and that if I was released from the county jail, he and the members who stood on principle and honored our code would be rewarded annually with what I could provide financially.

Hours later I was on the Grey Goose happily shackled because this was the ride to my freedom. The Grey Goose was an old, rusted transportation bus that had metal iron bars across the windows and faded blue paint. I did not care what I rode on, I was happy I was a ride away from my freedom. Yea, my freedom was finally in reach, in sight, and the topic of discussion.

My mind was in a frenzy, full of positive thoughts as I sat in my seat, feet shackled, hands shackled, but joyful to say the least. All the things I'd once taken for granted, I was now admiring and in awe. I looked out at the houses, cars passing, animals, and all the things I'd longed for after spending over twenty years in prison.

I was like a kid on their first road trip. I was excited just to see life outside of prison in the free world, and believed I was closer to my dreams. I silently begged and asked our Higher Being to allow me the freedom I so deserved.

After arriving at the Men's Central County Jail in Los Angeles, I realized how after being in a structured environment for so long, the times had changed the entire culture of this concrete jungle.

This place was foreign. Now I never underestimate nothing, but how I viewed certain inmates and sheriffs wasn't positive. I really didn't care being that my aim, goal, and motive was to remain focused on the blessing God had given me.

"Evidentiary Hearing"

My moms, sis, bro and the family joined me in thanking our Lord and savior for finally providing the day to prove my innocence. It was time for me to unwind and settle into my new living quarters. It had been 20 years since being in the county jail, so I knew it was mandatory that adjustments (mentally) fell in line.

Politics that I adopted from being on a Level IV prison yard were new to these youngsters in the county jail. Level IV was your maximum security level in a California prison. The politics and prison rules had been a lot different compared to lower-level custody yards.

Here in the county jail, there wasn't any structure, this environment was the true meaning of dog-eat-dog world. The young men in the county jail were fresh from being removed from the streets for whatever reason; this was an environment where the youth outnumbered elders and older men. Their mind state is fighting each other, gangbanging, and who will overtake a module (meaning the strongest gang module) and call it theirs.

In these times I advanced my mentality, status, and beliefs. I'm not on the Black-on-Black crime. While having lived in a maximum security prison, you realize regardless of one's gang ties, all that matters is race in the prison yard. Black, White, or Mexicans. That's it. Everything is segregated by Blacks, Whites, and Mexicans.

Critical moments can occur in a prison yard between different races; you wouldn't tell another Black guy to not assist you in dire moments, because of the color each tribe one claims. Being here in the L.A. County Jail, I was now in a different type of hostile environment where nothing was the same as I'd remembered. Survival instincts allowed me to adapt to my environment and remain alert to my current surroundings, while also remaining focused on why I was there to begin with.

I'm down here on some positive legal business, but in jail or prison the mass could care less about your blessings. Only a few concerned themselves with the importance of my legal fight. I wasn't tripping either. It's nothing for me to act a fool at any given moment here since I was aware of my 'dog-eat-dog' environment. The victim isn't a role I'm comfortable being in.

My myriad of visits kept me grounded. Also, the daily conversations with women and loved ones plugged into my consciousness and gave me the balance necessary to fight off the negative crowd, vices, and energy of the different and wild characters.

Some cells housed six grown men in a cage together often of mixed races, with no privacy, and only one toilet. The county jail was a filthy institution, not to mention the many diseases and viruses that are usually experienced in Men's Central Jail. Rodents run across the tiers, and you don't have the necessary cleaning items to maintain a sanitized and clean living environment. Due to the county jail receiving new offenders daily, it is an inhumane place to be housed.

It took me nine months sitting in that cesspool to eventually receive the hearing. The hearing consisted of the attorney general having his or her witnesses, and my lawyer bringing a witness (which is now a new discovery) in my own defense. Instead of a jury it's up to a judge to hear the case, ask questions, and in time render a verdict exhorting or exonerating me or sending me back to the slave quarters. The county jail stay was cool for the fact it allowed me to build and meet with a young relative I had never met in person, as well as my young homies.

Aside from that, the process with the court proceeding and hearing was just how it went 20 years ago. Even 50 years before it was still biased, ineffective, unjust, racially partial, and denigrating to those who unfortunately don't have the voice, support, or means to receive a fair legal hearing.

It was sad not just because I didn't prevail; it was bigger than me and my freedom. A win for me (justice served) would have afforded victory to those who were innocent like me but who could've gained hope by witnessing the system correcting their blind mistakes. To be denied freedom was a slap in my family's face as well.

My witness knew when he pointed me out and testified against me in trial that he was proceeding with callousness in his heart. 20 years later for whatever reason he wanted to right his wrongs which I respect, but the district attorney and judge couldn't respect that he was now testifying on my behalf. They couldn't exonerate this gang member, Black man, lower class citizen, even though it was the legal and moral correct thing to do.

The judge didn't look at me once throughout the hearing; instead he looked around me at everybody else, as if my presence was meaningless. Wasn't I the focus?

Finally, his pale face built up the courage to look my way and have the audacity to say, "Mr. Jones I see you've tattooed your face up."

I couldn't say anything back due to it being considered a clap back, which would sink me in deeper waters. This White privileged man would never understand my pain, scars, plight, or struggles. These tattoos symbolized all that, and I wore them with pride equal to that of an American soldier. I'm sure my eyes told him what my mind was saying, "F*ck you!"

As much as I wanted to vent about the proceeding, I took it in stride by turning around in my chair every so often to see the many supporters who took off work, woke up early, and sacrificed their time to be a witness to this blessing we all believed God was granting me. It was all my homegirls who I love like family, my uncle, sis, moms, my brother's baby mama, and a few comrades who rode this emotional wave with me.

The hearing didn't go in our favor. The attorney general, an Asian woman, chewed up our star witness and made his testimony seem incredible. Our witness was speechless on certain questions and his nerves were on edge, which led to a mental breakdown. It was bad and we knew it, but we felt like God would override the human debacle.

The judge ruled in the DA's favor and read 30 pages of legal bullsh*t about why he wasn't going to set me free. My head shook from side to side and bitterness was in my body, but I never dropped my head. I wouldn't dare show any sign of defeat in front of this man. He held the power to my physical freedom but God willing I'd never surrender my mind to anyone's power aside from my own.

I walked out the courtroom emotionally defeated. I asked God to give me strength to endure this current blow, give me the knowledge needed to overcome this legal plight, and to please give me the peace and understanding as to what was happening.

A volcano was brewing and usually I am wired to blow a dorm, yard, or a day room up when I am mad. As an older man my concept has changed. I can't let my emotions go unchecked. If anything, I felt I had to lead by example, so once I got back to Men's Central County Jail, I strolled back to my module stone-faced and concealing my feelings.

Where the f*ck was the White lady (psyche) when I needed her?

In here my motto has been to never let them see you sweat. One of my older homies who'd been an old cellmate in Folsom State Prison asked me what happened. He genuinely cared. He used to tell me when we initially connected, to stay on top of my legal work. He understood the trials of fighting a "life" sentence while trying to remain hopeful of regaining what was stolen from me.

My older homie only wanted me free, so his conversations were always naturally uplifting. Nobody wanted me free more than another innocent man who had his freedom snatched right from underneath him.

Now over 15 years later we were in the county together and I had to give him this f*cked up news. I searched his eyes and pierced his soul with words so real it'll cut through the hardest n*gga.

I said, "L these White folks would rather let an innocent man rot in here than allow me to become vindicated. It's 22 years incarcerated and they're bringing a lieutenant to my hearing to speak on my influence on the prison population regardless of it having no merit and being an injustice."

Anyway, I chunked it up to my homie (The B hand gesture) and told the sheriff to open my cell.

On God, once I entered that small one-man cell, I just let the built-up emotions run rampant. I was tired of being strong, tired of hoping, praying, and believing in God freeing me. I was tired of disappointments; basically I was broken spiritually.

Tears ran down the face of a man who didn't know tears existed. I just kept repeating to myself "Damn blood what do you want from me?", talking to my God.

My homies came to the cell and found themselves speechless. What do you say to a n*gga who has been bound to a Level IV 180 prison for an entire 22 years for a crime he didn't do? What do you say when he's been crucified for being ghetto raised?

You know my mother has always given me the words needed for any situation. This time even she was lost for words; there wasn't any logical reason for the judge's denial.

My daughter and brother surprised me in the crisis. They were the ones who spoke and breathed life telling me "keep it pushing." The strength you digest from a loved one can become contagious and infectious. It was all I needed in that moment to say "Y'all won that round, but we'll win the match."

During this time of rejection, I was reminded of my sister's words. Rasheeda often pointed out how my immediate circle feeds off my energy, so I am always conscious of the energy that I project. Nothing keeps me grounded more than hearing her voice in my head saying, "We are in this with you until the end."

I can't be selfish and give into the vices and denial from this White supremacist system.

I want to say to the ridas who lay on their rack, who lack support or may want to give up:

You need to expand your minds, go soul searching first, and recognize your elders who sacrificed and laid the foundational understanding; they had it way worse than us.

I always think of those on death row, the ones who have been down 20, 30 and 40 years in the SHU.

The ones who got killed in these sewers fighting for our human rights.

Hey "Homey," just know WE ARE RESILIENT people, and in America they'll forever have a bone to pick with us.

We can't always depend on our physical strength.

WE ARE INTELLIGENT enough to utilize our mental process to receive reparations, monetary gain, or plain ole legal justice.

Don't y'all ever forget it.

"We may encounter many defeats, but we must not be defeated!"
—Maya Angelou

Dated Fall of 2019

Wrongful Conviction of Omar Jones

People vs. Omar Jones

Freedom can be defined as the power or right to act, speak or think as one wants without hindrance or restraint, absence of subjection to foreign domination or despotic government, and the state of not being imprisoned or enslaved. As a 65-year-old mother I come bearing my heart, soul, and my unwavering faith to continue my quest for freedom for my son Omar Jones. Omar was wrongly convicted in 1999 of a crime in which he did not commit. I have sought consultation, advice, and have worked with some of the best lawyers in Los Angeles as it relates to my son's case. However, God, the judicial system, and the powers that be have had different plans. Today, I humbly come asking for support to assist with fighting for the freedom of Omar Jones for he is not guilty.

His loving mother, Cheryle Ms. Jones

CHAPTER 9:
HUSTLE AND MOTIVATE

MOE

My return to the belly of the beast has been the most challenging part since my initial incarceration. I've grown mentally despite what my prison record shows or what outsiders may think of me. To be held captive for twenty-plus years for a crime you didn't do is beyond human mistreatment. I've put my faith in God believing He'll set me free. To get that close to family and freedom and then get sucka punched by the same court has literally taken the spiritual strength out of me.

I'm one of the few from my generation who hasn't turned his back on the youth. During my own trials and tribulations, denials, losses, grief, and struggles I would still find time to give attention, advice, and support to the youngsters.

It's the same sad song, just a different day. They're coming to this prison yard with triple digit numbers, 100-200 years to life sentences. I'm old enough to be their father, uncle, or big brother. It is my duty to embrace them, educate them, and enforce the mental fight they'll need to withstand this oppression, until we win back our freedom.

I am continuing to work out my mind, body, and soul to ward off the stress that haunts me relentlessly now. I've asked God to give me a sign of what it is He wants from me. Until I change that, He may not answer my prayers.

During reflection period a female friend requested for us to engage in a fast. During this fasting process we fell out. I won't get into details, but I will say it got ugly. In the end, it became a blessing and a key part of my resurrection. It was as if God tore me down to build me back up.

I'm allowing God to work on me and trusting He'll be my strength. I just stay busy reforming myself by reading, writing, praying, studying, and educating the brain. Yes, I am so thankful to have a strong will. It's a daily struggle to remain hopeful and optimistic, and think and act positively. I've given too much time and energy to lost causes. I'm a father who has been absent for 26 years. I'll never be able to get that time back with someone I helped bring into this world; due to circumstances she was without me. My priorities are to my daughter, grandson (yes, I am now a grandpa), my moms, grams, sis, bro, and my remaining family.

I'll forever be grateful and loyal to the relationships built during tough times that are no longer physically present, RIP. I'm eager to establish a grassroots base where monetary funds can be issued quarterly to the kids of our homies who have died or been stuck in prison, but stood on honor and the integrity of the ghetto.

Since my incarceration I've experienced some moments that I am proud of. I've taken a Counselor 101 course. It's a goal of mine to become a motivational public speaker and work with troubled youth in places like juvenile halls, group homes, and placements. I am able to do that work here rigorously.

"We are all we got," is our motto.

I imagine once the platform is set up, I'll be able to network with people in high places who see the fruit of my labor. I envision connecting with those in the gang world who are productive and want better for our kids and communities. You see a lot of us behind these walls don't get credit for our consciousness, our change, our ideals.

They (the system) highlight our survival skills. What are we to do in an environment where violence is the norm? It's called self-preservation. Who's going to allow themselves to be a victim of rape, extortion, beatings, or death? Unfortunately, there are those who are not as strong. Until you've been here and lived here it's hard to judge the next person for defending their livelihood.

I would like to give myself credit for the ability to condition my mind to refrain from most negative thinking when facing an issue. I repeat, most negative thinking. It ain't easy. How can you expect positive, good blessings to come with doubt, pessimism, and negative results. Unconsciously we're guarded and only expect the worst-case scenarios.

My mom is my closest friend. We are clearly connected and linked in every emotional way. She can say or write words in a card that'll pull at my core. She and I talk, laugh, joke, and cry about life in general. She's been my comfort blanket during this storm. She rides with me right or wrong. She believes in me, and is the greatest hidden gem within me.

When people turn their back on me, she scolds me with, "You don't need them you have me, your brother, your sister, and grams."

Because of my mom's personal experiences that she endured decades ago and my own experiences, we're able to relate. We can speak on anything, and I am comfortable trusting her opinion. She has always told me to stand on integrity, be responsive, and to always remain true to my beliefs. She taught me that the women in our Dynasty are real on all levels. They've bred stand up men. We have an awesome relationship, and as we both age it has gotten better. We're aware that we should express our love every second, minute, and day because life is too short.

Her love is like no other. She's sacrificed her time, money, relationships, health, and happiness to see her children happy. My mom won't even vacation with my sister. Her argument is, what would she look like vacationing with me locked up? It puts guilt on me being that I am a standup man. I don't want my mom or nobody else to suffer over my incarceration.

Lately, I've been laying on my rack feeling that my freedom is near. God is mightier than this system and He will deliver me to my peoples. Until then it's another day up for this king. Before I head out, I want to acknowledge a few folks.

My daughter. My daughter and I are so much alike, it's crazy. I see a lot of myself in her. She's outspoken and isn't going to cut corners to avoid rubbing you wrong. She is naturally intelligent, articulate, and well-mannered. We sometimes let our pride and stubbornness get the best of us especially after a disagreement. She has no clue of the power she has over me. She can single handedly check me, those are the perks of having a daughter.

I love her smile, voice, laugh, and personality. She is such a strong, beautiful woman inside and out. She used to come and visit me before becoming a victim of a fast lifestyle which resulted in heavy consequences. We got through her hardship together. We wrote relentlessly and got closer emotionally.

I am proud to say she was released from prison and has transitioned into a working-class citizen, paying bills and living a slower life than before. She's given me my first grandchild, a son. And she even gave him my last name. The brilliance and charisma literally run in the family. We overcome and we refuse to let my incarceration strip away our love, loyalty, and support from each other. We've been through our ups and downs like most father and daughter relationships, but our love and commitment to each other is priceless.

Truth is, I've lived here with guilt over leaving my daughter out there fatherless. We know the struggles of women and young girls who get taken advantage of.

Daughter, I love you more than anything. Thank you for loving me despite my absence and thank you for loving me despite my flaws. Thank you for allowing my legacy to continue through my grandson.

My brother. My brother, my son, my lung, my cohort has taken the streets by storm in keeping our name alive. I didn't want this life for my little brother or my relatives who lost their life in the underworld. It has a strong hold that can't be avoided especially when it's in-house and consists of family members.

Due to our lifestyles, I've only been able to correspond with him through letters and phone conversations. I find myself overprotective of him and I'm critical of who he has in his presence. I know firsthand how people misguide, misuse, and don't have each other's best interest and I only want the best for him.

After losing our two relatives to gun violence it was up to my brother to hold our family down. Unfortunately, he did not have long to do so because at the age of 22 the slave chains overtook him, and the judge sentenced him to 12 years in state prison for a nonviolent offense. THE SYSTEM DON'T CARE ABOUT US!

I respect bro because he is very intelligent and could easily pursue a high-paying job, or graduate from school and climb the ladder to high places, like an executive or entrepreneur. God, please continue to watch over my bro. Give him the means necessary to care of his kids while enjoying the fruits of his life and labor. I love you bro. Never minimize your worth by sacrificing for n*ggas who don't know their own.

My billionaire relative, we needed you home. You taught me a lot. You were like a father and teacher to me. Like I told you in '98, if I could have done half your 30-year bid in federal prison, I would have. I love you that much. I couldn't have made it out there without you. Once you left, I went reckless.

You used to be my balance and tamed the anger within. Even though it went bad for me in my court hearing, I am optimistic about winning my freedom once the feds view my case. I always told my momma that whenever you would be set free, you'd do the footwork necessary to exonerate me. You are home relative, let's get to work.

RASHEEDA

If there was anything I was learning to appreciate more, it was becoming more at peace with my thoughts; how they determined my actions and how my actions were rooted in passion. That passion created this woman I have grown to love.

It had been five years since I'd proposed the idea to create a book for my brother and write about our life experiences, and what incarceration had done to us. Almost every time he called me from prison, he would ask me where I was with this book. Truthfully, every chance I got, I took the time to sit and write.

What was not easy is that life was still happening in the real world for me. As much as I would have liked to go on a sabbatical to write – accompanied with cozy socks, different flavors of teas, and watch the seasons change – the reality was I had to wear many hats at home and in my community. As we know, some good things just take time.

One evening, I was in bed scrolling my phone. I must have skipped through all my favorite Neo Soul artists, my Nipsey Hussle playlist, and the music I typically listen to when I need a mood booster. R&B is always my favorite. Out of nowhere "You Bring Me Joy" by Anita Baker began to play and it caught my attention.

"You bring me joy
When I'm down
Oh so much joy
When I lose my way your love comes smilin' on me
When you love me, I smile
I feel your heart and you feel mine
You bring me joy
You bring me joy
Don't go too far away
If I can't see your face I will remember your smile"

This song was beautiful. Now, I was not familiar with Anita. Yes, I said it. I did not have the luxury of growing up on Saturdays with the old school Marvin Gaye, The Temptations, Gladys Knight, etc. while cleaning, so my music buds lacked. But it was something about this song that warmed my heart.

I replayed the song over and over until I decided to read the lyrics. After reading the lyrics I didn't feel as connected because I had no current love interest. But as I continued to listen to Ms. Baker sing about love and joy with such a soulful angelic voice, I could not help to think of a universal love.

"What brings you joy Rasheeda?" I asked myself.

Then, I started to feel. I started to harmonize more.

"You bring me joy." Ahh, a universal love always made me think of my twin, my father, and of course Omar. So I began to think about them more, their faces and their smiles as I sang the sweet sounds of Anita Baker. As I continued to sing and scroll on my phone, the first thing I stumbled across was an old, dated text message from my dad.

It read,

"*Stand up and represent Rasheeda! Remaining apathetic and apolitical is the biggest curse and obstacle confronting our Black youth. Get and remain .... STAY involved, cause at any day & time it could affect you directly! Could be our moms, fathers, cousins, uncles, nephews, neighbors, church members, brothers, etc... ad infinitum' Love your spirit, activism, & concern. – Yo proud Father*"

As I played Anita to death that evening, I couldn't seem to shake my dad's text message or my brothers' images.

Stay involved Rasheeda!

What brings you joy Rasheeda?

Stand up and represent Rasheeda!

Continue to make your father, mother, family, most importantly yourself proud Rasheeda!

And so, I continued to do so.

Wearing many hats was not easy but as I mentioned before I felt I had a moral obligation and responsibility to do so. There was nowhere in history where I'd heard that my ancestors, freedom fighters, or leaders ever complained about the hats that they wore. They just wore them and did what they had to do.

Becoming more involved in Essie Justice Group allowed me to take my leadership skills to new heights. The more involved I became with the Healing to Advocacy Program, the more invested I was in healing for Black women. Before you know it, I'd applied to become a facilitator of the program and brought my mother, aunt, and a couple of my friends into the organization. I was elated that even my loyal Colombian friend joined.

This not only strengthened my leadership abilities, but really allowed me to bring women into a space that they needed. You were not judged at Essie. You share your story at Essie. You grow a sisterhood at Essie! It warmed my heart to be in the organization as a facilitator, especially with my mother and bonus mother at my side. As you grow in social justice organizations you meet new people who share the same passion but may have different fights.

During an event that was held with Essie I came across a young married couple who was holding it down in another area of social justice. The wife happened to also be a member of our Essie Justice organization. This couple was sharp. They were well informed. They had a powerful story to share. They were relatable but most importantly they were about the work to abolish prisons, patriarchal systems rooted in White supremacy, and ultimately teach our communities about our political power.

Sign me right on up! It didn't take me long to connect with the young couple who founded Initiate Justice. Initiate Justice's mission is to end incarceration by activating the power of the people it directly impacts. This meant empowering people in jail/prison and the communities that support them. Like my time at Essie, I had to engage in a twelve-week organizing program that taught me the basics of community organizing, policy, and advocacy. Basically, how to put your action behind your emotions; how to turn your pain into purpose and be a part of change.

As a social worker, I knew the importance of policy, but I never thought that as a Black woman, I, Rasheeda Jones would have a seat at the table. Initiate Justice taught me that not only did I have a voice, I had a seat, power, and influence. The organization believed in my work so much they allowed me to build out the healing circles alongside another member, to provide space for healing within the organization.

"When we heal, we win!" was our motto. Through Initiate Justice I was able to visit the California State Capitol and experience what it's like to be in those spaces. One visit turned into more visits at the Capitol, and over the years, I was able to share Omar's story and its impact.

"Omar is my brother. He was found guilty at 21 years old for a crime he did not commit. He has spent the last 25 years of his life in prison, a lot of the time in solitary confinement. Every day we fight for his innocence."

I shared my story to anyone who was willing to listen. I even shared it with people who did not seem to care. I was determined. With each visit, member, person I met, I took away something new and a different perspective. As I learned policy and the importance of navigating these spaces, I realized often it was bigger than Omar. My actions and voice would not only benefit Omar, but would also support every person who suffered from policies and laws that didn't have them in mind.

I remember my last visit to the capitol. I wore my 4-inch leather pumps, my Anne Klein pencil skirt dress, my Essie book bag, a pin with Omar's face on it, and I rocked my stylish cornrows.

Yes, I became confident enough to rock my cornrows around these folks! Needless to say, I had fashionably arrived.

The policy that the community members were informing assembly members on, was to vote in favor of a bill I found out had no benefits to Omar.

A lady pulled me to the side and said "Sis, I heard your story. I don't think this applies to your brother." My heart immediately dropped.

After all these years I never acknowledged that Omar was sentenced to two life sentences without the possibility of parole, meaning he would never get a chance to be placed in front of a parole board to review his charge. The devil is a lie! I thanked the lady for informing me, sucked up my emotions and still decided to go in with the people.

I began to speak with a heavy heart because again this did not apply to my situation. "I was 7 when my brother went to prison, and I am now 32. I have been advocating and dealing with this for 25 years. Although he would not benefit directly from SB 300, I mentioned it earlier – we are a community, a collective, and a village. When one wins, we all win. I just want to emphasize that again I am here in solidarity for all of us."

I could feel my nerves and my hands start to sweat as I gazed at everyone in their eyes. I then looked at the assembly member's assistant with direct eye contact and continued, "Congratulations, I am happy your uncle is coming home, and I wish that for all of our loved ones."

The assistant had mentioned before that she was also impacted with her uncle being incarcerated since she was eight. (Let me fill you all in on a secret. It does not matter what position you are in life. We are all impacted in some way by this system).

I looked to my left at a man who was just released from prison from serving a life without the possibility of parole sentence. He mentioned that he made a promise to give back his time and help free those left behind.

I affirmed to him, "I uplift you for coming home and being home and being the change."

My last words concluded, "I just want to again emphasize that if nothing else we are here humanizing our experiences."

I took a deep breath and, in that moment, I was reminded that it was in fact bigger than Omar and I.

Senate Bill 300 (SB 300) is a proposed law that would reduce the sentence for certain inmates convicted of murder. Specifically, it would allow inmates who are not the actual killer, but were perhaps an accessory to the crime, to be considered for parole release.

Leaving that space, I felt informed and empowered. I realized that my work would not and could not be solely for one person. It really takes a village.

My Village

My village consisted of me being a member of two organizations, a school social worker, and the best aunty in the world to my brother's children. My twin had blessed our family with three kiddos who, like Anita, sang and brought me so much joy, as did the students at my school.

I had asked God to provide me with a career that would allow me to get paid and feel like I never had to work a day in my life. So far it has served me well. My profession allows me to teach young Black students and families about the importance of mental health, while affirming their cultural identities in an effort to improve their academic performance.

Imagine that, I once lacked knowledge and cultural awareness but now I get to do things like introduce HBCUs and Black inventors, and love Black babies with no conditions. God sure did answer my prayer. This career has also allowed me to spend time learning about ways to be more supportive of Omar, while still following personal dreams.

I mentioned early on in this book that I always used writing as a getaway, an escape, a haven. Well with my new role in education and new knowledge of policy, my courageous spirit, and personal experience, I decided to write a book titled, *Justice.*

I took my personal story, the story of my nieces and nephews, and the students that I served and turned into a children's book. *Justice* is about a young boy who struggles with expressing his feelings about his father's incarceration, until one meaningful visit with his dad helps him develop enough courage to finally share the truth with his classmates. After discovering that he is not alone, he uses his experience to help his peers cope and normalize speaking out when in need of help.

With my newfound role as an author and educator I was becoming everything I needed when I was younger. I needed guidance, so guidance is what I gave. I needed someone to be present, so every session I was fully responsive and provided active listening. I needed patience, so now I always greet people where they are with a compassionate, soft, and assertive voice full understanding. I needed someone to sit down with me and connect a couple of dots to make more sense as life passed by. That is what I have tried to be for my students, my clients, my family, my friends, and my brother's children.

My brother's children are like mine. The way I love them is hard to describe. I've tried to do my best by exposing them to different ideas, perspectives, and experiences. Unfortunately, they too know what it is like to be subjected to long visits up north, prison vending machines, and memorable photos with their dad in prison. It has become a part of their story that they will tell one day.

While incarceration has been a part of their story, it has been a joy to teach them the other parts of their stories too; stories they can be proud of. For instance, I taught them that my paternal grandparents moved to Los Angeles with a seventh grade education and owned some of Los Angeles' most successful Black businesses. Yes, my grandparents owned a plumbing company, a theater, fish market, laundry mat, houses, and a Black-owned motel named after my granny. My Paw Paw employed many members from the community who just needed an opportunity and a chance.

I've also explored my maternal side of the family and the geniuses who birthed them. They were daycare owners, truck drivers, escrow officers, police officers, and proud city workers. Even down to their dad, uncle, and me who are now entrepreneurs, self-published authors, and hardworking leaders.

As I educated them about the greatness from which we came, I had an epiphany. As much as I talked about the challenges, losses, and heartaches that our family had to overcome, I could never let those overshadow the amount of noble and beautiful accomplishments that were made in the process, even if it was only temporary.

I digress, but there were so many more things that I find myself proud of lately. I'm proud that I embarked on engaging in more things that were not considered the norm. Like yoga, which taught me self-awareness and how to embrace the present moment with gratitude. I'm proud of the blog website I created to discuss the importance of mental health in the Black community, which has allowed community members to share their stories through creative writing. I'm proud that after so many years I reached out to my youth pastor and I started to attend church again. My religion is still something I am working on, but I know God and my relationship with Him is solid. I am proud that I've been able to create a balanced and successful life for myself and be a model to others in the process. In that, I have defined what success looks like for me and only me.

Rasheeda's definition of success: being happy and at peace with wherever you are in life. Giving it the best that I got.

I am proud that I have taken the leap of faith to fall in love with everything around me, including the process. I have embraced the love of friendships and romance, and love of community and myself. I really love the many communities that I represent in the purest form.

I am proud that I let my hair down and am not afraid to try different things, all while still styling and profiling. I am proud that I still seek adventure and I am not afraid to create more memories through traveling abroad, adopting new cultures, and meeting new people.

Egypt has recently been my favorite country out of the 17 countries I've had the opportunity to visit and be immersed in. I was able to pray at the great Mosque of Muhammad Ali in Cairo, Egypt that Malcolm X prayed at in August of 1964. To pray in the same mosque that Malcolm X prayed in with my dad's tasbih prayer beads in my hands, was a feeling of fulfillment to last a lifetime.

Wait, there is more. I followed in my cousin's footsteps and became a member of Delta Sigma Theta Sorority Inc. (oh, how it is every woman's dream to rock that crimson and cream). I was now a part of another sisterhood. This sisterhood embodied the same beliefs that I did, uplifting the Black community through public service and programs. Somehow, I kept landing in the love of the right people, where all the people felt like home.

I am proud to say that I even ran my first Los Angeles marathon. 26.2 miles, each mile dedicated to every year Omar has been incarcerated. The marathon symbolized health, wealth, and political awareness all in one.

Now, I never returned to "Superman" or my love in Atlanta, nor do I have my husband and beautiful Black healthy babies (yet); but when I say I have been living, I have been doing that while still being grounded in my why.

Rasheeda, how have you been doing it, they ask? Well, I found the love that ignited the fire that has been inside of me all along. Yes, I found the love that has been inside of me all along. I gave myself grace and have always stayed connected to the source, God.

I sit in my loft on my couch. It is surrounded by a creek with ducks, lots of trees, and a serene feel. It is the exact home that I asked God for, and it is mine. I sit here in silence as I hear the cars on the streets and watch the trees breathe back and forth out the skylight view.

I begin to reflect, "Everything that I have ever asked you for God, you have made happen for me. You have turned me from a girl to a woman with heartfelt experiences in between. You have blessed my mind, my heart, and my spirit. You have surely carried me along the way. God, I thank you for blessing my family. God, I thank you for blessing my friends. God, I ask that you continue to bless us. God, thank you for my home, peace, understanding, and patience. God, I ask that you protect us and keep us safe. God, I ask that you bless those who have transitioned in life. Remind them that their spirit lives on. God, I ask that you bless our communi . . ."

My thoughts were interrupted. Truthfully, I could go on forever talking to God. It gets like that sometimes. This time I was interrupted with a text from my bonus mom.

"Sheeda, I am going to be on a panel talking about my book, *I Did Not Sign Up for This* and guess who is going to be asking me questions?"

I texted back with excitement, "Who?"

"None other than Michelle Alexander, the author of *The New Jim Crow: Mass Incarceration in the Age of Colorblindness.*"

I became so excited for my mom. It would be a dream come true to be in the presence of the woman that started a deeper connection with my brother, my dad, and I. With no hesitation I congratulated my bonus mom and booked a flight to Newark, New Jersey to support her efforts.

My bonus mom spewed wisdom and gems that night and shortly after I met best-selling author Michelle Alexander y'all. She signed a copy of her book The New Jim Crow for me, and she left with a signed copy of my book *Justice* from me. Now how full circle is that?

The Outro

It has been a pleasure writing this vulnerable body of work. I've shared knowledge, I've shared truth, and I've shared vulnerability. Some things were difficult but necessary. I've created something with Omar that will surely make an imprint on our family, our children, our community, allies, and generations to come if they are open to receiving power and gems in the form of a book.

Before I go, I would like to leave with this:

To my twin, it has been an honor to share the same womb with you (I smile as I think of this). Only you and I know what it is like to be in mommy's womb together, be nourished together, grow together, and meet the world together just seven minutes apart.

It's something that I have never been able to describe to anyone about having a twin. For me, our love has just been different. You have always been my protector as I have been yours. You have always been my safe space and someone I was proud and happy to be a part of. Yes, you! You make me proud to be your sister.

I do not know exactly how life has made you feel but as your sister I have empathized with every part of your experiences. From the pressures of gang life, to witnessing things as kids we had no business seeing, I think what broke my heart is watching how life happened so fast.

We were innocently playing WWF wrestling, Barbies, G.I. Joe, Mario Kart, Madden, NBA Live and spending summers with Youth Services at Figueroa Elementary. Then in the blink of an eye the influences of cliques and gangs were all around us. If anything has hurt me more, it was you being taken away for so much of our lives. It was never the same for me without you.

But more importantly, there was always a worry about how life made you feel. I worried whether you were scared or afraid. Were you nervous or angry? Were you happy, sad, did you feel loved?

As adults those thoughts still occupy most of my mind, especially when my days are long. Some days I overthink, just wanting life to be good for you and everything that you touch. I pray deeply that there are moments in life that are good to you. Despite it all you have given me the best gift that I could ever ask for.

Allah blessed our family with three beautiful beings that call you dad. I love them deeply and whole heartedly because of you. They have brought so much joy to us, and it is because of you. Although this book is a memoir of our big brother and I, it was imperative that I dropped a message to you. You mean that much to me. Your authenticity, your spirit, your character, your heart, your wisdom, and leadership are undeniable. You have always and will always be deserving and more than enough. I pray to Allah He blesses you with abundance in this lifetime. I love you Oceans Full.

Mental Note: "None of you will have faith, believe, or truly love until he wants for his brother what he wants for himself."

– Prophet Muhammad (peace be upon him)

To my mother:

I know that Moe's absence has left a huge void in your life that no one can ever fill. However, you have done the best that you could and helped build a level of resiliency within us that can't be matched. Over the years there have been so many gems that I've adopted, and the most sacred gems come from the two beautiful souls that gave me life, you and my dad. I am because of you, be proud of that mommy!'

To the readers:

One of the most beautiful things in the world is using your love, power, and influence for the good of others, especially through service. I encourage you to become more informed by reading books, watching documentaries, or listening to podcasts. I empower you to learn where you come from by asking questions from elders that have been around. This will enhance the level of pride in your identity.

I charge you to use your voice and challenge oppression, policies, laws, and fight strategically like our ancestors who laid the blueprint. I ask that you prioritize your mental health by seeking support and therapy, connecting to like-minded individuals, laughing often, and crying when you need to. Please cry, this world is and can be cruel as hell, but you are the light.

Lastly,
Justice for:
every Black child, woman and/or man who suffered sexual, mental, and physical
abuse dating back to slavery.
Justice for:
every person who is sitting in a jail or prison cell for trying to make a way for
themselves and their families, trying to provide basic needs.
Justice for:
anyone who has ever been accused or wrongly convicted of a crime they did not
commit.
Justice for:
every person who was a victim of crime who never received justice.

Justice for:
every child or family who does not have adequate resources or care, including
housing, mental health access, food, career opportunities, or education.
Justice for:
every political prisoner and freedom fighter who died or was murdered for our
liberation.
Justice for:
every child or family member who has been impacted by all systems including a
judicial, foster, and/or social service system.
Justice for:
every Black and Brown child who has been a victim of the school to prison pipeline.
Justice for:
every person who has lost someone or something because of the oppression
and barriers we are up against daily.
Justice for:
every person who was a victim to police violence or murdered by the police.
Justice for:
every community organization, leader, or group that was ever infiltrated or
destroyed because of their love, fight, and dedication to the people.

Justice for:
every community who has experienced a genocide against their people and land.
Justice for:
anyone who has lost someone to gun, gang, or any kind of violence.
Justice for:
people who never received a chance or a second chance.
Justice for:
the millions of brothas and sistahs who stories are never told.
and
Justice for Omar.

As I depart, I am reminded that I have so much more love to give, experiences to make, freedom to fight for, communities to serve, children to teach, and significant stories to tell. I'll continue to do so if God allows me to see another day. But for now, I must go. I can't be late – I have reservations for Disneyland.

“What happens to any of us, anywhere in the world, had better be the business of all of us.”

- Mamie Till

AFTERWORD:

2024 UPDATE - A MESSAGE FROM OMAR

First and foremost, I want to thank, acknowledge, and surrender my all to the Highest, God. He's been my anchor, my strength, and my haven. He's been patient with my ignorance, disobedience, and lack of understanding. I am physically locked up in chains, but I am finally free spiritually. I feel my soul has been freed from its heavy burdens. God, thank you.

After regaining strength and breath from the system (criminal court building), I realized I needed to find resolve in what my future held. God sent me an angel. I was introduced to my wife through mere prayers. I asked God to send me a woman who'd love me for Omar Jones and not Mad Moe, an illusion of my true self.

God knew the woman I desired. She came into my life well-equipped with God's armor. From the jump she challenged me by seeking a higher version of self; she saw something in me that I was denying myself of, "mental advancement."

My wife and I recently established a clothing brand that we proudly call Wee the Future & Moe'sta Made. It is urban wear with positive logos, intended to impact our youth and communities. We have also created opportunities for aspiring models to model our brand, including children and adults.

I've reshaped my entire mind and flushed out a lot of old ways that came by habit. I've made myself more accessible to mental advancement by taking all the free self-help groups, attending college courses, and starving my weaknesses for mental growth. I've received a plumbing certificate and a life coach certificate.

I am currently working three jobs and on a waiting list to attend a substance abuse program which would certify me to teach and support abusers. These tools are equipping me and preparing me to survive in society after my release. I am in the process of co-writing a book with five comrades which will soon be published.

This prison I am currently at has opened doors as well. Certain nonprofits graciously come and help us fight our plights by bringing light and attention to our stories. Last year I was fortunate enough to sit down with my comrade J. Burton and speak on our injustices. I'd like to shout out the camera crew and non-profit, Between the Lines. Between The Lines' YouTube views hit the millions and has helped bring attention to my legal plight.

God has been good. He has removed old friends and put me in better mental and spiritual situations. Yes, I am incarcerated, but I am utilizing my time to aid the youth. If I'm not exercising my mind and body, I'm chilling with my wife, kids, grandson, siblings, and family. Before I sign out, I'd like to sound off with double salutes to all who withstand the pressures of racism, poverty, bigotry, and new era slavery (prison).

I've been incarcerated 26 years now, and there's not a second, minute, day, or night I am comfortable; I dread this torment. I'm the voice of the real letting all who's in reach know, ain't nothing about prison cool.

I lost a lot of loved ones who are resting in peace, and time that I'll never get back, like raising my daughter. By living life, even if in prison, I've gained a lot and now my eyes are on the sparrow.

I am happily married.

I am spiritually free.

I will never take anything else for granted.

Peace and blessings be upon y'all. I am checking out. I got work to do.

In love and solidarity,

Brother Omar Jones

ACKNOWLEDGEMENTS

I would like to acknowledge those who've made the sacrifice to educate me while giving me insight to eradicate my ignorant ways. Loyalty and the utmost respect for the G's before my time. Free the people still fighting this struggle.

-Omar

I would like to first give honor to God for everything. His love, grace, mercy, and for choosing us for this assignment.

To my beautiful family, my dear friends, colleagues, community members, villages, neighborhoods, and organizations that I represent. I wish I could mention you all, but I thank you as you played a significant part in my journey. My love for you all has no bounds and I am forever thankful for the genuine and intentional love, care, concern, and support throughout the years.

Brandon Scott, I could not have completed this project without you. It was tough but you stood with me. I am filled with gratitude for you as a writer, visionary, and friend.

Mr. Jones, as a proud sister and best friend, I am honored to have had the opportunity to develop a solid relationship that has flourished, despite being 300-800 miles apart the past 26 years of our lives. We've held each other up and held each other down. My heart still speaks volume when we chant, "Justice for Omar."

-Rasheeda

ABOUT THE AUTHORS

Omar Jones

Omar Jones is a father, son, brother, husband, advocate, scholar, author, and a loving individual to many. He has spent the past 26 years in a California State Prison educating himself, working, and reforming his mind, body, and spirit for the freedom that awaits him.

Rasheeda Jones

The Los Angeles native is a psychiatric social worker, mental health advocate, activist, writer, and author who is passionate about bringing positive change, advocating on behalf of others, and inspiring others to be the change they wish to see in the world. She also serves as a community organizer with Essie Justice Group, advocating for women and families affected by incarceration.

Embodying her various roles as a devoted daughter, sister, aunt, loving friend to many, Rasheeda's ideals and vibes spews the importance of viewing the world through an Afrocentric perspective.

Justice 4 Omar; Los Angeles, 1996

Omar age 2; visiting his father with mother and big sister in Ohio Prison, 1978

Omar and little brother visit California Prison, 2001

Omar and only daughter, California Prison, 2009

Omar & Rasheeda California Prison, 2012

Mother, Omar, & Rasheeda California Prison, 2017

2019

2019

2023

WHAT'S NEXT

If you've found your way to this page, it brings me joy. It shows that you've delved into this memoir and gained a glimpse into our world.

If you're feeling unsure about how to support us or get involved, here's how you can help.

1) Your voice is crucial. It doesn't matter where you're from, what you've experienced, your occupation, age, gender, race, and or your socioeconomic status. Your voice and presence have the power to create change. Use your power for good.

2) Take the initiative to educate yourself about the issues and concerns affecting your community, country, and the world. Focus on issues that directly impact you, and if none do, identify topics that captivate your interest. Having just finished this book, you can make a direct commitment to contributing to the end of mass incarceration. Take action by following, joining, or connecting with community organizers or organizations dedicated to addressing this vital social issue and supporting those affected by it.

3) Remember to always stay informed about your community, local, and state representatives. They play an essential role in pushing forward important bills that can lead to significant improvements and changes in laws and policies. Take the initiative to find out who your representatives are by using tools like "Find your (state) representative."

4) Recognize the impact of sharing information, lobbying, writing letters, campaigning, protesting, boycotting, petitioning, and making phone calls. It may appear overwhelming, and you might feel short on time, patience, or motivation, but understand that everyone has a role in the movement, and every action, regardless of its scale, brings us closer to the goal—one step at a time.

5) Emphasize the significance of providing care instead of confining individuals to cages. It's essential to humanize people's experiences and actively seek or generate resources to offer them the assistance they require. At the very least, stay informed.

I'm confident that the information shared will be useful because there are always opportunities to take action and raise important issues.

If you want to support Omar, you can make a difference by sharing his story, discussing it within your network, and familiarizing yourself with his case. You can also sign a petition in his name with the potential to reach California's Governor's desk. Additionally, writing letters to encourage Omar or sharing uplifting words during challenging times can have a positive impact. Whether you are a legal professional or have connections to individuals in the criminal justice system, policymakers, or advocates for second chances, your support could be instrumental in helping secure Omar's freedom.

www.ingramcontent.com/pod-product-compliance
Lightning Source LLC
Chambersburg PA
CBHW060708190726
48289CB00002B/595

* 9 7 8 1 9 4 5 8 7 3 1 7 1 *